D1258796

# The Third Circle

*Interactions That Drive Results*

Max Isaac

Anton McBurnie

# From 3Circle Partners

3Circle Partners works with businesses that are looking to enhance value by driving better performance and/or maximizing their investments in improvement programs. Our customized approach will accelerate your organization's performance through strong leadership and strategy, solid internal processes for superior execution, and effective interactions.

# Acknowledgments

We would like to thank Sue Reynard, Ed and Janet Taylor, and Carole Johnson for their invaluable contributions to this book.

PUBLISHED BY BRIDGE PUBLISHING

ISBN-13   978-0-9862956-3-8

Phone: 877-333-3606 or 416-483-7380

# CONTENTS

Preface ................................................................. 1
   Answering the "How" Question ................................. 2
   What Shapes Behavior? ......................................... 4

# PART I
# The Need for Individual Mastery

Introduction ......................................................... 9

1 —Recognizing Our Blind Spots ...................... 11
   Mental Models ................................................. 12
   Single- and Double-Loop Learning ....................... 17
   Moving Beyond Our Limitations .......................... 18

2 —The Impact of Leadership Styles ................ 21
   9,1—The Task-Oriented Leader ......................... 24
   1,9—The Country Club Leader .......................... 27
   9+9—The Paternal Style .................................. 30
   1,1—The Impoverished Style ............................ 34
   5,5—Middle of the Road ................................. 37
   9,9—Team-Oriented Leader ............................. 40
   Grid Styles and Single-Loop Learning ................... 44
   What We Can Learn From the Grid ..................... 45

3 —Can Leadership Be Defined? ..................... 47
   The Inherent Leader ....................................... 48
   Prescriptive vs. Learning Models of Leadership ........ 52

4 —The Struggle to Be a True Team Leader .............. 55
   Challenge #1: Double-Loop Learning ................... 55
   Challenge #2: Striving Towards the 9,9 Ideal ........... 63

**5—Creating a Feedback-Friendly Environment** .......... 67

**Conclusion to Part I** ................................................ 73

# PART II
# Team & Organizational Effectiveness

**Introduction** ........................................................ 77

**6—Managing Your Sphere of Influence** ...................... 81

    1. Decision Making/Planning ................................83

    2. Capitalizing on Team Members' Abilities............................84

    Determining Preferred Roles................................87

    The Oiled Cog................................................88

**7—The Strong, Silent Hand that Shapes Behavior** ...... 89

    Understanding Organizational Habits .........................90

    How Norms Develop ......................................92

    Changing Team and Organizational Norms............................97

**8—Levels of Change**.............................................. 101

**Conclusion** ...................................................... 105

    Sustaining Organizational Level Change ................................ 109

**Bibliography**.................................................... 111

**Index**.......................................................... 113

# Preface

*Consider the [Eckhard] Pfeiffer episode. The pundits opined ... that his problem was with grand-scale vision and strategy. Compaq's board removed Pfeiffer for lack of "an Internet vision," said USA Today. Yep, agreed the New York Times, Pfeiffer had to go because of "a strategy that appeared to pull the company in opposite directions."*

*But was flawed strategy really Pfeiffer's sin? Not according to the man who led the coup, Compaq Chairman Benjamin Rosen. "The change [will not be in] our fundamental strategy—we think that strategy is sound—but in execution," Rosen said. "Our plans are to speed up decision-making and make the company more efficient."*

*You'd never guess it from reading the papers or talking to your broker or studying most business books, but what's true at Compaq is true at most companies where the CEO fails. In the majority of cases—we estimate 70%—the real problem isn't the high-concept boners the boffins love to talk about.*

*It's bad execution.*

**— Excerpt from "Why CEOs Fail"**
**Ram Charan and Geoffrey Colvin**
*Fortune 6/21/1999*

CHARAN AND Colvin's article was a wake-up call for anyone trying to improve their leadership skills, no matter whether they were a novice supervisor or an experienced CEO. For years, even decades, the experts had told us that the most critical leadership skills were mobilizing the troops around a clear vision and having a winning strategy. Our job was to clearly communicate where we wanted to go, then trust our employees to find a way to get there. As Charan and Colvin point out, it's becoming increasingly clear that we need to put as much *or more* emphasis on implementation.

Charan and Colvin are far from alone in this belief. In a follow-up commentary on their article, for example, consultant Tom Curren described a two-year research effort by McKinsey and Company that identified nine mistakes responsible for 80% of the failures of significant change efforts. One of the nine was a lack of focus on performance, another was poor strategy. The remaining seven all dealt with aspects of poor implementation.

## Answering the "How" Question

Unfortunately, pointing out the problem is about as far as most experts have gone. They tell us the goal—to merge strategy and execution—but don't say how. (See Figure 1)

### Figure 1: Key to Leadership Success

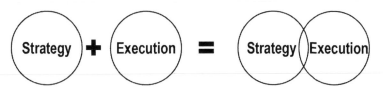

*We all want to merge Strategy and Execution—
The question is HOW?*

You have to read between the lines to find the answer. Here's Charan & Colvin again: "So how do CEOs blow it? More than any other way, by failure to put the right people in the right jobs—and the related failure *to fix people problems* [our emphasis] in time." And Curren: "Not distinguishing between decision-driven and behavior-dependent change. Creating higher performance always requires a mix of decisions (e.g., changes in business portfolio, market positioning, pricing) and behavior change (changes in skills, culture). *Not understanding that behavior-based change requires a very different mindset and different leadership skills results in more languishing change efforts than just about anything else* [emphasis ours]."

In other words, the answer lies in behavioral issues, and, more specifically, in creating effective interactions throughout the organization. Effective interactions are the linchpin behind both development of effective strategies and execution of those strategies (see Figure 2).

### Figure 2: The Three Circles Model
*Behavior as the Linchpin of Effective Strategy and Execution*

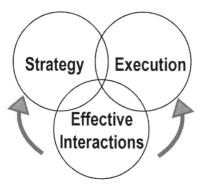

*Creating behaviors that foster learning and growth*

What we know is that...

- The quality of thinking around **strategy** is influenced by the kinds of **behavioral interactions** that occur within the organization. For example, a turf war between two key departments within an organization negatively affects the quality of the strategic thinking and the commitment levels in that organization. The imposition of a task-oriented manager's decision will affect willingness to execute the task.

- The quality and substance of behavioral interactions will affect **execution**. Experienced strategic planners know that lack of commitment within an organization (what people choose to do and not do) is as great a challenge to implementing a strategy as is the quality of the strategy itself.

- Even companies that emphasize execution spend a lot more time identifying the **physical elements of change** (getting new equipment, designing new processes, developing new forms) than thinking about the behavioral implications of that change. Rarely do we take the time to analyze the impact of the change on people ("who will be required to change how they work?") or to develop specific plans for gaining commitment ("how can we involve others in helping shape how the new changes will be implemented?"). Instead, the new practices are simply dumped into the organization with an unspoken prayer that all will go well.

If a strategy isn't aligned with execution and highly functional behaviors then almost any initiative will have limited success. This resistance to "flavor of the month" fads is a natural response to top-down initiatives that have no buy-in throughout the organization. A lack of buy-in is, in turn, a symptom of inattention to what influences behavior in the organization. Rather than getting commitment around their great new idea, leaders end up with compliance and passive resistance; for an initiative to become "the way we do things around here" it has to integrate all three components of the framework.

## What Shapes Behavior?

A manager enters a vice president's office with bad news: sales have dropped for the second quarter in a row. How the vice president deals with the situation—his or her leadership behavior—and whether that behavior is successful in helping the organization move forward is shaped by many factors. Beyond the basics, such as knowledge of market forces that may have contributed to the downturn, this VP's reaction is also influenced by...

- **Beliefs/attitudes** about people in general and this manager in particular, about what motivates people, about what gets the best results
- **Personality** type
- **Organizational norms** that create expectations about acceptable behavior
- **Knowledge** of the best way to achieve personal and organizational goals
- **Skill** in applying that knowledge

The fact that behavior is shaped by all these factors makes it hard to come up with a simple definition of what leadership is or should be. An approach that works for one person might not succeed for another. What is appropriate in one situation or company won't necessarily succeed in another.

These fundamental truths reside at the core of this book. You aren't going to find a list of leadership skills that you can check off one-by-one; you aren't going to find a list of rules or guidelines that will guarantee leadership success. Instead, you'll discover how to become more aware of your behavior as a leader and develop more effective strategies for dealing with the leadership challenges you face daily.

We've divided the book into two parts:

**Part I: Developing individual mastery in leadership.** Increasing your effectiveness as a leader has to start with understanding your own strengths and exposing your blind spots so you can build on the former and manage or compensate for the latter. Chapters 1 through 5 explore some basic strategies for improving leadership knowledge and skills, and set the groundwork for your personal work on improvement.

**Part II: Translating individual gains to organizational effectiveness.** Having a better idea of what you want to accomplish as a person is a great first step, but by itself is insufficient to bring about change. To be successful you need to involve the people around you not only in providing feedback on how your behavior affects them, but also in working on their own skills so the organization as a whole can become more effective. Chapters 6 through 8 explore how group dynamics influence behavior.

Over the years, we've been amazed at how often business leaders at every level operate at much less than their potential. Instead of creating energy and commitment around them, they are surrounded by seemingly intractable problems and mired in destructive personality conflicts. In this book, we explore factors that prevent you from being a more successful leader, and describe specific ways in which you can create an environment that promotes continuous personal and professional growth.

# PART I

# The Need for Individual Mastery

# Introduction

A SENIOR VP has just picked one of his direct reports (Marsha) to work closely with him on a critical, high-visibility project. Doing well could mean a career boost for Marsha; doing poorly could hinder her chances of advancement.

Put yourself in Marsha's shoes: you're excited about the opportunity; believe that you can contribute; have a compelling interest in making sure the project succeeds for both personal and corporate reasons. If you were Marsha, what kind of working relationship would you want with your boss to make sure this project comes off well? You'd probably come up with a list such as...

- Having both you and the VP treat the project as a priority and focus on deadlines and outcomes

- Having the boss treat you with respect and listen to your ideas

- Being able to speak your mind freely

- Sharing knowledge with each other to reach the best possible solution

Most people would come up with a similar list. In fact, we've asked people to write down exactly this kind of list and you'd be amazed at the consistency.

But as we all know, relationships between bosses and subordinates don't always meet these criteria. And let's not point fingers: truth be told, most of us would probably fall short if we were to hold up a mirror to our own management practices and behavior.

If most of us share a vision of an ideal collaborative relationship between bosses and employees, why do such relationships occur so infrequently? Is it because deep down we think that collaboration and respect are too pie-in-the-sky for the real world? Or is it that the way in which we *intend* to behave is often different from how we *actually* behave?

You'll be exploring the answers to these questions in the following chapters. You're going to be challenged to face your own mental models and assumptions, and given some tools for working through leadership challenges. This section provides you with background information that will help you understand your own behavioral history and assumptions, and develop strategies for improving your own skills.

# 1

# Recognizing Our Blind Spots

*At the start of a four-day workshop on leadership, the CEO of a specialized equipment manufacturer was put into a workgroup with what he considered were the smartest people in the company. Supremely confident that his workgroup would prove to be the best, he was shocked after the first exercise to discover they had scored the worst... and stunned when the same thing happened again, and again. As the week progressed, he became increasingly distraught: "I just don't understand what's going on here," he said repeatedly. "We should be winning."*

NONE OF us really understood at the time just what a profound experience the workshop turned out to be for this CEO. He truly believed, to the very depth of his being, that the best way to get good results was to bring together a bunch of very smart people. Obviously he was taken aback when people he considered "second tier" outperformed his "first tier" group by working together more effectively to produce superior results.

Few of us are as extreme as this CEO in our views, but we all have beliefs and mental models that shape our perceptions. And we *all* have blind spots that prevent us from being more effective leaders. This CEO held his beliefs for a long time until he was abruptly confronted with hard evidence that he could be wrong.

What's the secret to becoming aware of our blind spots? We can gain some insights through the work of Chris Argyris of Harvard University on mental models and true learning.

## Mental Models

Victor was a senior executive in a multinational organization with billions of dollars in revenue. He had a strong need to be right all the time. Whenever someone else came up with an idea, Victor would find a way to negate the validity of that person's point of view. His bosses knew about this problem: they had sent Victor to training courses and given him considerable input about his behavior over a period of years. Yet nothing changed. All efforts to create some self-awareness in Victor failed.

Events came to a head when Victor became the Corporate Director for a major strategic effort and began reporting directly to the CEO. While in theory he was in charge of all the Division Coordinators, those people still reported to their Division Presidents, not to Victor. As a result, Victor felt that while he was receiving some degree of compliance, none of the coordinators was going *the extra yard to ensure the success of this major strategic initiative.*

*Victor's first impulse was to ask the corporate CEO to speak to each Coordinator and demand greater effort, but a colleague talked him into a completely different strategy. Instead of making demands on his subordinates, Victor asked them for input on **his** behavior. He called a meeting where he said, "I'm feeling that as a team we're not doing as much as we could. Is there anything I'm doing as a leader that is getting in the way of your motivation?" The ensuing frank discussion proved to be a watershed, a growth experience for all involved. The outcome was much greater cooperation and effectiveness across all the divisions. (There may have been even better ways for Victor to phrase his question, but as a first attempt at inviting feedback, this wasn't bad!)*

These gains came about because Victor was persuaded to risk changing his **mental model**, the inner dialogue he had in his head about why people were behaving the way they were. Originally, he was very mistrustful, believing that the divisional champions were deliberately trying to sabotage the new corporate initiative through inattention. After listening to the division coordinators, he realized those assumptions were wrong, and had to acknowledge that he had sometimes acted in ways that stifled their creativity and discouraged them from taking any initiative. His experience can teach us a lot about how managers sometimes act in ways contrary to their own purposes. In Argyris's terms, Victor was being challenged to shift from employing **Model I assumptions** to employing **Model II** assumptions.

## *Model I assumptions*

Victor's original mistrust is a classic reaction based on what Argyris calls Model I assumptions, where people assume they must…

- Remain in unilateral control
- Win, not lose
- Suppress negative feelings
- Emphasize rationality

Because he assumed he could not trust people, Victor had strategies based on…

- Controlling the environment and tasks
- Controlling others
- Protecting himself and others
- Controlling access to information

These strategies tend to produce defensiveness and reduce openness because one-sided control is inherently contrary to producing valid feedback. Inadvertently, Victor was helping to create organizational dynamics that caused people to…

- Deal with conflict by avoiding or suppressing it
- Mistrust bosses and peers
- Play it safe; conform rather than question or create
- Save face

- Engage in win/lose inter-group rivalry; compete instead of cooperate

- Provide unquestioned obedience rather than informed consent

- Not invite feedback that would genuinely confront their actions

- Avoid public testing of ideas (especially those which may be important and threatening)

An environment dominated by these Model I assumptions and behaviors gives rise to ineffective behavior and problem solving. Because there is no open discussion of the conditions or sources of problems...

- Hunches become self-fulfilling prophecies. (If someone distrusts people, others sense this and react negatively towards that individual. This confirms the individual's mistrust. Eventually this notion is so firmly embedded in the individual's behavior system that it is almost impossible to change.)

- Valid information is a rare commodity; people will be honest only about trivial issues or unimportant problems.

- People are fearful of or discouraged from pushing their boundaries; learning is limited within a narrow scope.

People tend to become locked in their own perspectives and defensive of their positions, rather than trying to see situations from another's standpoint. These unproductive behaviors and consequences are the result of the natural **defensiveness** that all of us experience to some degree. We are all protective of our own reputation, fearful of being perceived as inadequate, especially when the stakes are high. We feel compelled to control the flow of information and to avoid opening ourselves to criticism. These behavior patterns become so ingrained that we are completely unaware of how we approach problem-solving situations.

## Model II assumptions

By having the courage to expose himself and his group to open dialogue, Victor was able to help steer his group towards more productive behavior. Over time, his basic beliefs slowly changed to what Argyris calls **Model II assumptions,** where people assume:

- They don't know everything

- Broad input is the best way to make good decisions
    - Seeking diverse sources of information (people and data) is the best way to develop valid information
    - Stakeholders should be invited to help make the decision

- The consequences of a decision are not pre-ordained
    - Therefore decisions and their outcomes must be monitored and observed to see if the assumptions were valid and the course of action effective

- People are intrinsically motivated to do well and contribute
    - A leader's job is to find ways to encourage intrinsic commitment to a decision or course of action

These assumptions can evolve only when people overcome their innate defensiveness, and no longer feel the need to protect their domain or live in constant fear of appearing less than perfect. People programmed with Model II theories of action produce group and organizational dynamics where:

- People feel comfortable inviting others to confront their views and challenge them on their assumptions

- Views/opinions/decisions actually change as a consequence of dialogue and an examination of all valid information (including observation, facts, and feelings)

- People avoid mind reading (presuming they know what people are thinking and why); reaching conclusions based on observable data
    - Presumptions are shared and openly discussed ("Are you saying that because...")

- New concepts are open to scrutiny by those who will use them

- One-sided control is rejected
    - Those affected by a decision are involved in making it
    - Those who have to implement a decision or operate a process are asked to help define, document, and improve their work

- People resist the temptation to save face at the expense of group productivity

If the values and behavioral strategies just outlined are used, the degree of defensiveness in individuals, within groups, between and among groups will decrease. Free choice will increase, as will feelings of internal commitment and contribution. As a result, problems are solved in such a way that (a) they remain solved, and (b) people are eager to participate in future problem-solving efforts.

A leader with Model I programming, in contrast, is more likely to ignore the ideas, knowledge, and/or experience of others when solving a problem. The "solution" will therefore likely overlook important factors—increasing the chances that the problem will recur—and the people involved in solving the problem will learn that their efforts and energy aren't really wanted after all.

## Single- and Double-Loop Learning

The outcomes of Model II behavior are consistent with how Argyris defines learning: *the ability to achieve the goals we intend to achieve and to solve the problems we intend to solve so that they remain solved permanently.*

This definition is much more rigid than the typical use of the word "learning." In the general sense of the word, we may learn something about cooking or sailing or improvement by reading a book. But reading alone doesn't meet Argyris's criteria: we haven't achieved the goal of actually cooking a meal, sailing the boat, or generating improvement.

On a much larger scale, many organizations bring in outside consultants to solve a problem... but when the consultants leave, the problems often reappear because the *organization* hasn't learned how to permanently solve problems on its own.

True learning, in the Argyris sense, will appear as *observable* changes in our behavior, our processes and methods, our ways of thinking. It requires knowledge as well as experience. And when we "learn how to learn," the result will be dramatically improved ability to solve complex, critical problems collaboratively.

Argyris concluded that Model I and Model II assumptions and subsequent behavior patterns greatly affect the amount of true learning that can occur within an organization. He described very different learning cycles associated with each of the models, as discussed below.

People operating in a Model I mode don't question whether they are making the right assumptions or have all the information. They become defensive whenever their values or judgments are questioned. They therefore operate and learn solely *within the confines of their values and untested assumptions and perceptions.* This leads to ineffective problem-solving and decision-making, and causes them to repeat mistakes.

This cycle occurs because the defensiveness associated with Model I behavior drives what Argyris calls **single-loop learning**: making decisions based solely on our own opinions and knowledge, without objective means of telling whether we're ignoring important information. Model I (single-loop) learning is therefore really anti-learning behavior:

- The underlying causes of problems remain hidden and are often undiscussable; problem solving about technical or interpersonal issues is ineffective.

- There is little or no public testing of ideas: not only are problems not discussed, but individuals will not ask questions to test their assumptions or conclusions.

- Very little feedback is provided to or by individuals as they interact.

A particularly pernicious aspect of these dynamics is that individuals operating in a Model I mode are unaware of the negative consequences of their behavior. They will state what appear to be Model II values (**espoused theories**), while their actions (**theories in use**) will be pure Model I—and they'll be totally unaware of this contradiction.

In contrast, Model II assumptions create what Argyris calls **double-loop learning.** People operating in a Model II mode assume they don't have all the answers. They are therefore open to receiving input, particularly on how their own behavior affects the achievement or non-achievement of the desired results. They encourage dialogue, help expose entrenched problems, use open, honest discussion to root out the underlying causes of problems, and engage others in finding permanent solutions.

The difference between being a single-loop learner and a double-loop learner is like the difference between controlling a thermostat and a two-year-old child. A thermostat will never question the temperature you've set. A two-year-old will always question your assumptions!

## When Defensiveness Is Too Big a Barrier

All of us have an innate defensiveness, a desire to protect ourselves from unpleasant situations or consequences, to ensure that we always appear in a favorable light. Most people are able to overcome the limitations that this defensiveness puts on their ability to succeed as leaders simply by being aware that it's there and to be expected, being open to feedback, and, most importantly, being willing to try out new behaviors.

For some people, however, especially those who operate in overdrive much of the time, their behavioral patterns are rooted so deeply that even if they know it's a problem, they have difficulty developing new ways of thinking. Still others can't even acknowledge that their behavior is hindering their personal and professional success. Exploring the roots of defensiveness is beyond the scope of this book. If you would like to learn more, reading the works of Albert Ellis, Aaron Beck and other seminal thinkers in the exploration of Cognitive Behavioral Psychology is recommended.

## Moving Beyond Our Limitations

Leaders who base their actions on Model I assumptions and make decisions without truly listening to input from others will forever be limited by their distrust and narrow vision. People who start to move towards Model II thinking and double-loop learning can more easily expose the root cause of problems; they will be in a better position to understand how they, their thought processes, and their behaviors either encourage or hinder effective problem solving.

This kind of probing is essential to efficiency and effectiveness in organizations today. With better and more regular feedback, people will truly learn about errors and improvement opportunities. The end result will be:

- Improved effectiveness in decision-making and policy-making

- Improved effectiveness in the monitoring of decisions and policies

- Improved problem-solving capability

## Chapter 1 Summary

- It is impossible for any individual to be fully aware of the impact of their own behavior.

- Our mental models shape our behavior.

- Model I assumptions and behavior are based on mistrust and defensiveness. They stifle creativity and lead to single-loop learning in which people are limited to their own perceptions.

- Model II assumptions/behavior are based on trust. They create double-loop learning, which allows leaders to move beyond their own blind spots and take full advantage of the skills, knowledge, and creativity of everyone around them.

# 2

# The Impact of Leadership Styles

$A$T SOME point in your career, you've probably been exposed to leaders whose overriding priority was to get the job done. You may have felt pressure (not all of it bad) to get work done, but more than likely your energy and attention were distracted by the need to anticipate what your boss was thinking so you could be sure to deliver what she/he wanted.

Or you may have encountered the other extreme; the leader who is so concerned for people that it seems nothing ever gets done. The most important criterion for this leader is to make sure everyone feels good about a decision or the workplace in general. While you're keenly aware of an impending business deadline, this leader is saying, "Where shall we hold Maggie's birthday party?"

These extremes illustrate two basic leadership behaviors described in seminal studies conducted after World War II at Ohio State University and the University of Michigan:

- **Initiating structure behavior** (concern for production): the leader clearly defines the leader and subordinate roles, establishes formal lines of communication, and determines how tasks are to be performed.

- **Consideration behavior** (concern for people): the leader shows concern for subordinates and attempts to establish a warm, friendly, and supportive climate.

Robert Blake and Jane Srygley Mouton developed these ideas further by looking at interactions between individuals, with an emphasis on how power and authority are exercised and how conflict is resolved. They realized that the two behaviors—concern for production and concern for people—were not opposite ends of a continuum but independent variables. That meant a leader could exhibit varying degrees of both initiating structure and consideration at the same time. Blake & Mouton ended up scoring leaders on a scale of 1 to 9 for both of these behaviors, and framing the results in their classic **Managerial Grid** (see Figure 3).

## Figure 3: The Managerial Grid

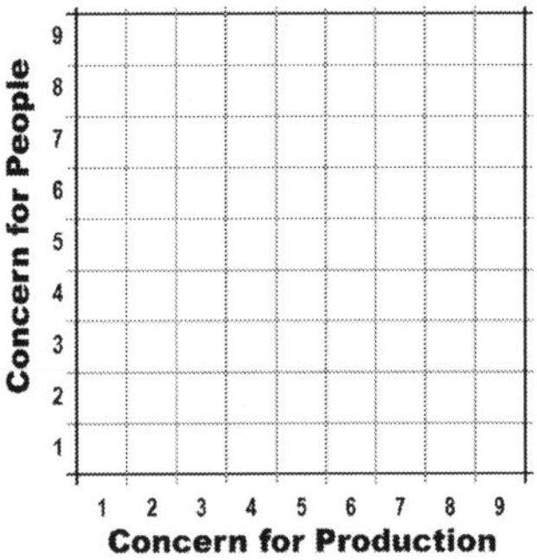

The fact that the two axes are grounded in solid research adds considerable credibility to the Managerial Grid. It creates a map of management styles that influence how effective interactions will be. We will highlight six styles of management that illustrate the extremes on the Grid (see Figure 4). Five of the six styles are easily located on the Grid by numerical codes that reflect their position on each axis; the sixth style, as you can see, represents a combination of two others and is therefore depicted as a see-sawing arrow.

## Figure 4: Management Styles

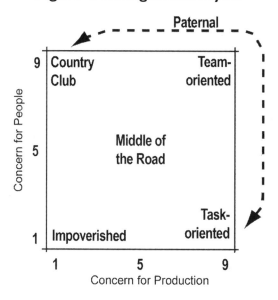

As a way to help you compare and understand differences in the styles, we'll look at four standard elements of leadership for each style:

1) Decision making

2) Conflict resolution

3) Balancing advocacy (seeking to have *your* viewpoint understood) and inquiry (seeking to understand *others*)

4) Giving and receiving feedback

In each category, we've provided examples based on real people and real behaviors, but keep in mind that these were chosen to describe the extremes on the Grid.

## 9,1—The Task-Oriented Leader

*"The Task Master"*

*Having just landed a major new contract, an elated Phil called his manager, Renee, with the news. "I've got some great news, Renee," he said. A curt "Yes?" was all he heard in return. "We got the contract!" Renee was silent a moment then said, "Okay. I've got to get back to my meeting now." Phil hung up with a sense of deflation.*

*This interaction was typical of Renee. Outside of work, she was known for her sense of humor. At work, she was all business. Pop your head into her office, and it was clear she resented the interruption.*

Renee's behavior is characteristic of a manager whose concern falls at the 9,1 position on the Grid: **high concern for production** (getting the job done) and low concern for people (see Figure 5).

This focus on work is manifest in numerous ways, both large and small. Take Fred, for instance. Like Renee, he was known as a smart, kind man… outside work, that is. At work, he was famed for merciless attacks on junior staff, often in public. Nothing really mattered to Fred but making sure the job got done right (meaning how he defined it). "Results at any cost" was his motto.

## Figure 5: The Task-Oriented (9,1) Leader

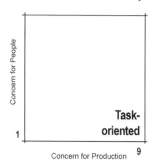

The low concern for people shown by leaders like Renee and Fred arises from the assumptions that people need to be compelled to work, that they can't be trusted to do it right, and that there is a contradiction between the organization's need for results and employees' desire to work in a friendly, supportive, congenial atmosphere. To a 9,1 manager, going "soft" is the surest way to sabotage business results.

The need to achieve results and be in control lies at the root of this style. Task-oriented leaders want to either do things themselves or direct others like pawns in a chess game. Since they have pretty much determined how something should get done, employees know that any request from such leaders for input is superficial, merely a pretense.

People working for such individuals learn to be compliant and "do as the boss says." Most people end up being very resentful of such leaders. Others may withdraw and become alienated. The highly competent individuals who are mobile and can choose to work in a more productive environment simply leave. In today's economy this loss of intellectual capital can make the difference between business success and failure.

The fact that people are merely compliant with and not committed to decisions or initiatives is an important disadvantage of 9,1 task-oriented leadership, especially if the task-orientation style becomes endemic to an organization. In the post-industrial, knowledge-based economy in which we now operate, gaining true commitment of our employees is critical. People who feel committed are likely to be more interested in learning and growth, bring more energy to the workplace, and stay longer with your organization.

Entrepreneurial individuals, though usually highly talented, are prone to developing a task-oriented, command-and-control style of management. In the early stages of a company's growth, this "big fish in a small pond" style can be highly successful, but the management literature is littered with evidence that as the company grows and the brilliant individual can no longer control everyone, the organization fails. Wise founders find more balanced, experienced executives to deal with the resources in the organization, while they find a role that utilizes their unique strengths.

On the standard dimensions of leadership, here's how a task-oriented leader performs:

1) **Decision making:** The task-oriented boss usually makes all the decisions, does not bother with trying to get buy-in … then afterwards wonders why implementation is poor. Subordinates lose interest in being innovative or creative and either become dependent on having a boss make all

the decisions or become resentful and, in extreme cases, even resort to sabotage.

2) **Conflict resolution:** Task-oriented leaders typically adopt a **win-lose approach** in addressing conflict (where they must always *win*). They will *suppress* conflict related to business issues, confident that they already know what is right. (Ironically, the suppression of useful conflict is supplanted by a lot of conflict around personalities.)

3) **Balancing advocacy and inquiry:** Task-oriented leaders are big on advocacy of *their* opinions, with little interest in others' opinions or reasoning. After all, why would a

---

### Summary of Task-Oriented Leaders

- Getting results is the paramount concern.

- Winning and being right are very important. Proving the opponent wrong and "winning" by forcing others into submission becomes the characteristic modus operandi.

- Can be very exacting taskmasters.

Our experience suggests that many North American managers who reach the senior ranks are task-oriented leaders. It's not all that surprising—after all, they are driven to achieve results. The question is at what cost and over what horizon. Employees may push to achieve a short-term result, but will lack the commitment or energy to sustain those results in the long term.

---

person who has the right answers need to understand someone else's point of view? Inquiring would only waste time that should be spent on getting the job done.

4) **Giving & receiving feedback:** Task-oriented leaders are not open to receiving feedback. But since they typically have strong opinions, they will freely give "feedback"… usually in the form of harsh criticism. A task-oriented leader's maxim is often "kiss up, kick down."

## 1,9—The Country Club Leader

*"The Nice Guy"*
*Larry was just the opposite of Renee and Fred: he believed that the best way to run a company was to keep people happy. He knew the detailed family histories of all his staff, and chatted every day with most of them. The first agenda item at his staff meetings was more likely to be planning the latest morale booster than selecting a new marketing strategy.*

Larry is an archetypical **Country Club** leader (upper left corner of the grid, see Figure 6, next page) who has a **low concern for production** and a **high concern for people**. A deep, almost missionary-like concern for people can prevent these individuals from understanding that these lofty beliefs don't always hold true, and distract them from dealing with pressing business concerns.

## Figure 6: The Country Club (1,9) Leader

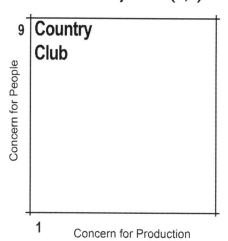

Because they evince a genuine interest in people, Country Club leaders are usually seen as "nice guys." What's not immediately obvious is an insidious assumption underlying their behavior: the belief that people are fragile. If people are fragile and need to be protected, they cannot be fully independent, functional members of a team or organization. That's why a Country Club leader sees him- or herself as a protector or barrier between "his" (or "her") people and the organization.

On the standard dimensions of leadership, here's how a 1,9 Country Club leader performs:

1) **Decision making:** For 1,9 leaders, a decision isn't right until everyone feels good about it. They will seldom make unilateral decisions, preferring to give everyone a chance to state their opinions as a way to gain buy-in.

2) **Conflict resolution:** Leaders with this orientation typically dread conflict (it disrupts their happy families) and attempt to **smooth over it**. Or they may use humor to deflect conflict. Country Club leaders downplay tough issues, accentuate the positive. They may also use substitute activities (such as organizing the holiday party) instead of dealing with critical issues. The ultimate outcome among their coworkers and staff is extreme frustration because the underlying issues are never dealt with.

3) **Balancing advocacy and inquiry:** Inquiry in the Country Club style of management will tend to be shallow. Asking tough questions that may call into question the positions presented by more assertive or aggressive individuals may be avoided in the interests of maintaining harmony and avoiding rejection. Similarly, Country Club leaders will tend to avoid strong advocacy because they don't want to impose their opinions on the group.

4) **Giving & receiving feedback:** Because Country Club leaders are attentive to the needs and feelings of others, feedback is very important—but it will likely be restricted to people's feelings and superficial comments: "How did you feel about that?" Because they want to smooth over conflict, they won't probe into controversial or sensitive areas. In giving feedback, they will want to be gentle, to appear helpful not critical. They love to give positive feedback, telling people how wonderful they are, and will avoid telling people when there is a problem that needs to be addressed.

Meetings under this style tend to be feel-good sessions where the emphasis is on building a motivational, warm family atmosphere.

This leadership style—wanting people to feel good, avoiding difficult issues—creates unhealthy group dynamics. Since group harmony is paramount, people will be very unlikely to make even the mildest criticism of another group member. When faced with negative feedback or poor performance, a country club individual or group will **externalize**: blame factors other than themselves for the problem. (Externalizing is common in all the Managerial Grid styles, but often is the most evident in the Country Club orientation.)

The Country Club leader's sensitivity may be coupled with a need for approval and a fear of rejection. (Contrast this

---

### Summary of 1,9 Country Club Leaders

- Harmony and good feelings are paramount

- People issues take precedence over business/task issues.

- Likely to be "thin skinned" and upset by conflict.


A Country Club leader will often defer to bosses or other people with authority instead of standing up for his or her beliefs or in support of his/her staff. When combined with a protective approach towards subordinates, the result is a non-challenging, perhaps even stifling, work environment. People may grow bored, frustrated, or even resentful.

---

approach to that of the Task-oriented leaders, where there is very little regard for the reactions of others. Getting the job done is what counts. With the Country Club leader, being accepted is far more important.)

## 9+9—The Paternal Style

*"Dad (or Mom) Knows Best"*

*Jessica was proud of the fact that she came up through the retail business the hard way. She never completed a college education, but did well in her career through hard work and persistence. Take a walk through any store carrying her company's product and Jessica would quiz you in an aggressive way: "See this aisle display? What's wrong with it?" All the time, you knew she had the answer ready at hand.*

*This attitude kept Jessica apart from her employees and she liked it that way, liked being on a pedestal. At the same time, she was very protective towards her people. If you were loyal to her, she'd be loyal to you.*

Viewed from afar, you could be tempted to describe Jessica as an ideal leader: she had a high concern for getting the job done (like a task-oriented leader), but also displayed a lot of caring and concern for people. The trouble, however, is that her caring was tempered: like a Country Club manager, she believed that people are fragile and need protection. This combination of task-orientation and a Country Club concern for people is the profile of a Paternal leader. (And here's one instance where we can't bow to the gender police: paternal has a much different connotation than either maternal or even parental.)

It's difficult to portray Paternal leaders on the Managerial Grid because *they aren't really combining* a high concern for people and production; rather, they tend to hold the two extremes in a delicate balance as shown in Figure 7 (hence the odd numerical notation of "9+9" associated with this style).

### Figure 7: The Paternal (9+9) Leader

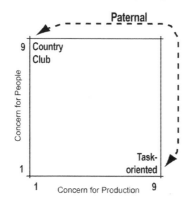

It is relatively easy to distinguish a pure Task-Oriented leader from the more caring, yet equally controlling, Paternal orientation. The intentions of a Task-Oriented individual are very clear. You always know where you stand: "It's my way or the highway." The Paternal style has a manipulative feel to it. The Paternal leader alternates between Country Club benevolence and a controlling, "I know better," superior attitude that tends to place the boss on a pedestal and make subordinates feel like children. (This also contrasts with a true 9,9 Team orientation, described below, which is characterized by an adult-to-adult approach in which a genuine respect for the individual is used to focus on achieving results through mutual collaboration.)

On the standard dimensions of leadership, here's how a 9+9 Paternal leader performs:

1) **Decision making:** Most decisions are made by the Paternal boss. Having already determined the best course of action (the controlling element of the relationship), he or she may then provide warm encouragement and coaching to make people feel good about implementing it.

2) **Conflict resolution:** The Paternal leader exerts an often-subtle control over conflict, tending to **suppress it** much as a task-oriented leader would. The difference is that Paternal leaders may allow subordinates to argue amongst themselves, only to come in at the end and, like a benevolent parent, settle matters. A common pattern of behavior is to disown a subordinate should conflict continue. A rewards-and-punishment pattern of interaction can evolve between a Paternal leader and his/her subordinates.

3) **Balancing advocacy and inquiry:** Jessica exhibited a very typical Paternal pattern of false inquiry around business issues: asking questions to which she already knew the answers. It is almost guaranteed that the other person will supply a wrong answer, allowing the Paternal leader to correct the subordinate and reinforce the idea that she/he is all knowing. (Paternal leaders use true inquiry only for non-business issues, demonstrating concern for people

by asking about their personal lives.) In advocating their position, Paternal bosses will often state opinions as if they are facts. This pattern of speech can be very intimidating, inducing a sense of inferiority in those lacking confidence in their own point of view. Over-explaining and repeating their views is a way in which Paternal leaders make quite sure subordinates "get it."

4) **Giving & receiving feedback:** Paternal leaders believe it is part of their job to provide corrective feedback to subordinates, but they have no reason to think that those subordinates would have valuable input for *them*. Feedback is therefore a one-way street, always coming down *from* them, never coming back up *to* them.

The combination of task-orientation and Country Club concern is deadly. People who report to Paternal bosses grow more and more dependent. They will hesitate to accomplish things until and unless they are sure they have the boss's approval. They want to avoid incurring the boss's displeasure. This stifles truly independent thinking and leads to imitative behavior. As with the pure task-oriented leadership, Paternal management often creates a boss-think dynamic where subordinates learn to feed to the boss what he or she wants to hear.

This stifling environment is reinforced by the Paternal boss's ability to induce guilt in subordinates. When a subordinate steps out of line, the boss may induce feelings of guilt by either overtly or subtly letting the subordinate know of his/

her displeasure, which in turn reinforces the need for others to go along with the boss-think.

---

### Summary of 9+9 Paternal Leaders

- A pendulum swing between concern for getting a task done and wanting people to feel good about a decision is the hallmark of a Paternal leader.

- Quite often are very sensitive to perceived lack of loyalty. This can be combined with a "family" approach in which values, as defined by the boss, are stressed. As a paternalistic leader, Jessica is likely to treat well those people who are obedient and compliant (rewarding behavior she values), while being hard on those who resist, disagree, or don't show her the proper deference.

- Boss-think becomes so automatic that those involved are quite unaware it is occurring. It is not unusual to hear a paternalistic boss complain that capable subordinates keep checking in or are risk averse. Just as an overprotective parent can stunt the growth of a child, a Paternalistic leader limits the development of subordinates, ultimately leading to resentment on their part.

---

# 1,1—The Impoverished Style

*"Stay out of the firing line"*
*We have all met people like Chuck. At one time, he was one of the CEO's favorites and rose high in the organization. Then, as new people came on board, he slowly lost favor and began losing position and power. Today, he has no real authority, no concern for either production or people. He's just trying to survive until he can retire.*

The main driver of the 1,1 Impoverished "leader" (see Figure 8) is simply survival; the principle concern is to maintain a place in the organization until she/he can get out or until the environment changes.

## Figure 8: The Impoverished (1,1) Leader

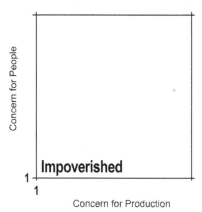

The phenomenon of Impoverished leadership often occurs in two circumstances:

1) **As a result of restructuring and layoffs.** It is a very easy step to move from the kind of dependency that

a Paternal management style fosters to a survival mentality when someone's job is threatened. Over the years, many individuals come to depend on their organization for their sense of self-worth. In the more ruthless times of today, these individuals resort to an easy escape from facing up to their own vulnerability by becoming problem employees. They operate in a survival mode, with low concern for production and low concern for people.

2) **In reaction to a strong task-oriented culture.** A powerful task-oriented boss elicits predictable reactions from his subordinates. The strong individuals leave; those who are insecure or susceptible to co-dependent relationships remain. Those who stay are often emotionally beaten into adopting an Impoverished survival strategy. In this scenario, compliance is seen at its extreme.

On the standard dimensions of leadership, here's how a 1,1 Impoverished leader performs:

1) **Decision making:** People operating at the 1,1 level are loathe to bring attention to themselves or assume responsibility. Non-involvement is the key. They will seldom take the lead on a decision or ask others to get involved in decision making.

2) **Conflict resolution:** Involvement of any kind, including conflict, is avoided.

3) **Balancing advocacy and inquiry:** If your goal is to be noticed as little as possible, you will not want

to inquire into others' feelings, beliefs, or opinions. Similarly, you'd be reluctant to take a position on anything, often preferring to table issues, fearful that acting on something may produce bad results and then you would be held accountable.

4) **Giving & receiving feedback:** The approach here can be summed up in two words: "why bother?" Most 1,1 leaders are concerned with survival, not with improvement. They would not bother providing feedback to others; nor would they be particularly interested in hearing what they should do differently.

Some Impoverished leaders are quiet mice that go through the workday unnoticed, sitting in the back corner at meetings,

---

### Summary of 1,1 Impoverished Leaders

- Low or no concern for accomplishing results

- Appear to go through the motions

- May appear busy, but that activity won't be directed at important business-related work

- Likely to appear as either quiet mice or be problem employees


People who operate with a 1,1 Impoverished style are usually surprised at their level of non-involvement—possibly because they often shed their non-involvement the moment they leave work and become quite active and involved in other pursuits (hobbies, civic interests, volunteer work, etc.).

---

never saying anything of substance. Others are much more disruptive, ready to complain about anything and everything, using whatever manipulative strategy they can devise to disrupt or interfere with the work. It's easy to imagine them in the guise of rebellious teenagers: "This is stupid. I don't want to be here."

# 5,5—Middle of the Road

*"Compromise Is the Answer"*

Oddly enough, one of the most telling characteristics of a Middle-of-the-Road manager is that no one will have any complaints about them! Take Tonya, for instance:

> *During a feedback session with Tonya and other managers, no one had any suggestions for how she could improve. Tonya was viewed as very smart, very caring, and totally reliable. The limitations of her style, though, were revealed through a bit more digging. Though highly respected, Tonya wasn't viewed as inspirational. She always played things safe, settling for "good enough" and never strongly pushing an idea. So while she was certainly a competent and well-liked leader, she wasn't really as effective as she could have been at getting the most out of her staff, nor did she progress as far as she might have in her career.*

Mouton and Blake and others have studied behaviors in organizational settings using the Grid as a framework and have linked the Middle-of-the-Road orientation (5,5; see Figure 9) to a profile that is quite familiar—that of the "organization person," the individual who has learned to live within a system and has learned to play the politics necessary to survive. In Grid terms, the Middle-of-the-Road individual has learned to *balance* the needs of production with those of people, rather than *integrate* them as in a Team Leadership (9,9) orientation.

### Figure 9: The Middle-of-the-Road (5,5) Leader

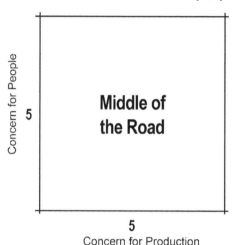

On the standard dimensions of leadership, here's how a 5,5 Middle-of-the-Road leader performs:

1) **Decision making:** Playing it safe is the hallmark of 5,5 decision making. They are quick to use mechanical methods of decision making (such as voting) so as to avoid the tension that comes from constructive conflict as part of decision-making (see below). In decisions related to goal setting, they will often take an incremental

approach—"what can we submit as a goal that will keep head office happy... a 10% revenue increase should do the trick"—versus seeking a true understanding of their work unit's capability and setting stretch goals to inspire people.

2) **Conflict resolution:** At the root of this orientation is compromise as a way of **avoiding** conflict. As soon as conflict becomes uncomfortable, the Middle of the Roader will seek compromise or use mechanical methods, such as voting, to bring about a quick resolution.

3) **Balancing advocacy and inquiry:** Interaction tends to remain at a superficial level in a 5,5 orientation. A politeness can creep in which robs the team of its dynamism. There will be a certain amount of advocacy and inquiry, but it will lack the incisiveness that is evident in a 9,9 orientation.

4) **Giving & receiving feedback:** The 5,5-oriented leader will strive to balance negative and positive feedback, often by *sandwiching*—giving a positive comment prior to any negative feedback. The receivers of such feedback soon learn to recognize this facet of the 5,5 leaders style. They wait for the other shoe to drop whenever a positive comment is made.

Our own experience in trying to identify the Middle-of-the-Road orientation suggests that it may be linked to an exaggerated discomfort with conflict. Individuals with this orientation have a real desire to achieve results, but it is tempered with a discomfort in situations in which the advocating of strong beliefs or positions may lead to conflict. A manager using this style tries to achieve a balance on the basis of "you have to give a little to get a little." For example, when trying to balance the needs of all the parties involved in a budgeting process, a Middle-of-the-Road manager would set budget targets at a level that would satisfy corporate staff while not upsetting the business unit management.

In some cases, Middle-of-the-Roaders are individuals who slipped into a 5,5 style after being influenced by the culture in which they worked (e.g., a bureaucracy). After starting out as new employees with boundless enthusiasm, they became jaded mature workers; a change that crept in imperceptibly over time. Once alerted to this situation, a 5,5-oriented individual can be inspired to greater dynamism.... Unfortunately, such gains are often short-lived as the person once again seeks the comfort of balance.

---

### Summary of 5,5, Middle-of-the-Road Leaders

- People with this orientation will always try to create balance. There is a constant striving to not rock the boat too much and to maintain the status quo.

- A "safety first" approach characterizes the 5,5 leader's comfort in the status quo.

- Individuals with this orientation may be seen as having well-honed political instincts.

---

# 9,9—Team-Oriented Leader

*Leaders of Integrity and Authenticity*

If you asked anyone in Miguel's company what they think of him, almost everyone will tell you he's doing a great job. (A few strong task-oriented managers will say he is too soft.) In fact, Miguel is by nature a charismatic 1,9 leader, very concerned about the people who work for him. After his recent promotion to second-in-command, however, he rapidly developed an equally strong commitment to the business.

Staff find it easy to support Miguel because he not only says that he'll do whatever is best for the company—he does it. For example, the CEO recently threatened to fire a key engineer who had behaved badly. Though Miguel didn't like the engineer personally, he knew that engineer was critical for bringing their product to market on time. So he stepped in to resolve the conflict.

If Miguel has any fault, it may be his 1,9 roots. He is much more likely to speak up to the CEO to resolve a people issue than to challenge a business assumption or decision. Overall, though, employees like and respect Miguel. They always know where he stands, and can tell that his actions are consistent with his professed beliefs. He works tirelessly on behalf of the company, but also takes a real interest in the people around him. As a result, he has an indefinable authenticity that has won him extraordinary loyalty and commitment from employees.

With the recent integration of business acumen with his existing people skills, Miguel is coming ever closer to the 9,9position on the Managerial Grid (see Figure 10).

### Figure 10: Team-oriented Leader

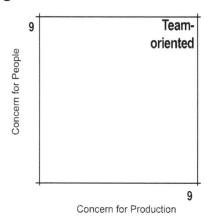

His story is important in many respects:

- First, it demonstrates the way in which a concern for people can be effectively blended with a concern for production to achieve a highly effective 9,9 orientation

- Second, it shows that each of us will need to take a different pathway to becoming a 9,9 leader based on where we're starting out. In Miguel's case, he had to temper his concern for people with a greater interest in getting the work done

- Third, Miguel is proof that not only can't we be "perfect" 9,9 leaders, but that we don't have to be in order to be effective

Here's another example of the third point: A woman executive started out as a highly aggressive 9,1 task-oriented leader.

Through education and exposure to the Grid ideas and other leadership principles, she was convinced to try changing her behavior. She never truly lost her abrasive edge, and never become very skilled at the "people stuff." But though she was awkward in dealing with people, her genuine caring and respect for employees and her dedication to the business allowed her to become a very effective leader and a dynamic part of the organization.

In contrast to the 9,1 and 1,9 leaders, people operating with a 9,9 orientation assume no inherent contradiction between organizational purpose and the needs of people. The mantra of the 9,9 leader is:

> *Work is accomplished by committed people, focused on the same goals, who have the skills and tools to be effective. Interdependence through a "common stake" in organizational purpose leads to relationships of trust and respect.*

On the standard dimensions of leadership, here's how a 9,9 Team leader performs:

1) **Decision making:** As leaders implement the 9,9 orientation, they become aware of a universal tendency for those in positions of control to underestimate the need to communicate and involve others in decision making. The 9,9 leader realizes that a major responsibility of any leader is to galvanize all of the resources available to reach high quality decisions that:

   – Involve those impacted by the decision
   – Generate commitment rather than compliance

- Are done at a speed that meets the needs of the situation

2) **Conflict resolution:** Team-oriented leaders recognize the importance of healthy conflict in spurring creativity and surfacing the underlying sources of problems. They deal with conflict openly, and use effective facilitation techniques to create an environment where people can be open about problems and concerns. Any conflict that arises is more likely to be around genuine differences in opinions about business issues, not about people or personalities.

3) **Balancing advocacy and inquiry:** A 9,9 leader sees advocacy and inquiry as two of their most important skills because it is only by drawing information out of others (inquiry) and clearly stating their own opinions/reasoning (advocacy) that discussions can address the truly important issues. Further, strong advocacy and inquiry skills help us become better double-loop learners.

4) **Giving & receiving feedback:** Strong 9,9 leaders excel in stimulating continuous improvement by valuing the giving and receiving of honest, candid feedback. They not only invite feedback, but respond to it (demonstrating by their actions that they are truly listening to others).

---

### Summary of 9,9 Team-Oriented Leaders

9,9 leaders are the antithesis of the typical ego-driven leaders. They try to do their best with respect to the needs of their work units/teams while at the same time striving for the best possible results. These attitudes help instill in others a desire to do the best possible job. True 9,9 leaders:

- Genuinely invite, encourage, and respond to feedback

- Are willing to deliver feedback to others in a constructive manner

- Foster a desire to continuously develop both individuals and the organization

- Always seek win/win solutions

- View healthy conflict as a vital ingredient in creativity

- Treat failures as learning opportunities

---

## Grid Styles and Single-Loop Learning

As examination of Blake & Mouton's leadership styles and Argyris's Model I and II assumptions and behaviors reveals many connections. For example, all of the Grid styles (except 9,9) exhibit some degree of Model I assumptions:

- Remain in unilateral control

- Win, do not lose

- Suppress negative feelings

- Emphasize rationality

The consequences of those assumptions—which are a product of the defensiveness we all experience to some degree—are also present in those Grid styles. People working under Task, Country Club, Paternal, Impoverished, or Middle-of-the-Road leaders will tend to…

- Deal with conflict by avoiding or suppressing it

- Mistrust bosses and peers

- Play it safe; conform rather than question or create

- Save face

- Engage in win/lose inter-group rivalry; compete instead of cooperate

- Provide unquestioned obedience rather than informed consent

- Discourage feedback that would genuinely confront their assumptions and actions

- Avoid public testing of ideas (especially those which may be important and threatening)

Team-oriented leaders, in contrast, strive to act based on Model II assumptions:

- They don't know everything

- Broad input is usually the best way to make good decisions

- The consequences of a decision are not pre-ordained

- People are intrinsically motivated to do well and to contribute

As a result, open dialogue, honest discussion, and effective problem-solving are much more likely to appear under 9,9 leaders.

## What We Can Learn From the Grid

The descriptions of the various Grid styles are not meant to pigeonhole people or imply that leaders act in only one of these styles. In fact, Blake & Mouton are clear that all of us use all or most of the different styles at different times, depending on the circumstances. Similarly, it is not necessary or possible to always have the introspection required to effectively execute double-loop learning, a basic requirement of 9,9 leadership.

Still, the 9,9 approach represents an ideal or preferred alternative that we should always be striving for, because that's when we'll be best able to maximize organizational resources to achieve results. Double-loop learning leads to fundamental solutions to problems, whereas single loop learning (characteristic of the other Grid styles) is likely to lead to symptomatic solutions that often have unintended negative consequences.

By studying the Grid in conjunction with single- and double-loop learning theories, we become more aware of behavior (our own and others) and its effect on personal, team, and organizational effectiveness. These ideas help us do a balcony check—observe our own and other's behavior from afar, as if on a balcony above the fray—and provide the kind of input that allows us to become lifelong learners.

Studying the Grid confers another advantage: we become more aware of the traps that we and others are prone to fall into. If you are a natural 1,9 Country Club leader with the defensiveness routines that accompany that style, you'll have to remind yourself to consciously check whether you are ignoring important business needs or deadlines.

Keep in mind, however, that the Grid is not an all-encompassing leadership model. It focuses primarily on attitudes, beliefs, and consequences with a nod to some key skills (such as inquiry). It does not address personality factors—such as introversion/extroversion, stable/anxious, left-brain/right-brain orientations, etc.—commonly measured in personality tests, or try to prescribe personality traits that leaders should or should not have (a subject unto itself and beyond the scope of this book).

That said, the Managerial Grid has some very practical uses. More so than many other leadership models, it describes specific counterproductive leadership behaviors and how they contrast with the Team Leadership ideal. Once we know where our behaviors tend to fall on the Grid, we have a map that allows us to navigate towards greater leadership effectiveness.

## Chapter 2 Summary

• The Managerial Grid describes the extent to which leaders act based on a concern for production and a concern for people.

• The 9,9 position on the Grid defines an ideal of Team Leadership that balances both concerns. The 9,9 behaviors incorporate Model II assumptions and double-loop learning.

• Other leadership styles are based to some extent on Model I assumptions and single-loop learning.

• Most people use different leadership styles at different times. Each of us will have to find our own pathway to Team Leadership.

# 3

# Can Leadership Be Defined?

*Several years ago, a large organization decided to make "improving leadership" a key strategic initiative to improve overall effectiveness. They selected about 20 top managers that were widely considered to be highly effective (well-liked by peers and subordinates, able to meet goals and deadlines, etc.). Each of these managers was interviewed by behavioral experts, who identified specific strategies or tactics that made these people successful. The experts also interacted less formally with a number of managers at the other end of the spectrum. They then came up with a description of the "ideal" manager, a list of competencies and attributes that every manager should have.*

*Once the company had this list in hand, they used it to re-construct their performance review system. Thereafter, each manager was rated using a scale of 1 to 5 on how well she/he did against each of the competencies: in theory, the better they rated on those attributes, the closer they were to being an effective manager.*

IT MAY not surprise you that this system failed within a year. For one thing, it could not account for the quirky managers who somehow lacked the ideal attributes but who nonetheless delivered brilliant results. For another, the whole system soon became politicized, subject to the whims and opinions of senior managers who changed the list to fit their personal biases. In addition, it led to stagnation: people were only recognized for an attribute if they exhibited it in the way it was described on paper.

Interestingly, a paradoxical outcome of this approach was that the best leaders almost invariably scored lower on the attributes than their peers. Why? Because the subordinates of these leaders felt comfortable giving *honest* feedback. People working for, say, a 9,1 task master were not about to say anything detrimental about their boss.

This company's experience illustrates one of the biggest challenges around improving leadership effectiveness: how can we improve something that is so hard to define? One of the most contentious areas in leadership theory is whether there is actually a set of skills or capabilities that distinguishes "leaders," and whether these skills are innate or can be learned. Let's explore that controversy for a moment.

## The Inherent Leader

Some experts believe that leadership cannot be *developed.* That is, you either have inherent capabilities or you don't. Warren Bennis, one of the gurus in this field, states, "Leadership is character and judgment... and these cannot be taught." This view is supported in part by the work of Henry Mintzberg, author of *The Rise and Fall of Strategic Planning*. Mintzberg delves into brain research that analyzed how the left and right hemispheres of the brain influence decision-making. He provided examples of brilliant entrepreneurs who *intuitively* know what strategies to pursue—they were born with "what it takes" to be a good leader.

Other experts have adopted a slightly different approach, trying to identify a select number of components that identify outstanding leaders. Take, for example, the research of Bernard M. Bass and Bruce Avolio, whose work has revealed a continuum of leadership styles that describes how leaders interact with their subordinates. Here are three key points along their continuum, along with characteristic behaviors of those styles:

### Laissez-Faire Leadership

- Avoidance: The leader delays action. Authority is unused. Responsibilities of leadership are ignored.

### Transactional Leadership

- Creating contingent rewards: The leader gets agreement on what needs to be done and delivers rewards only if the assignment is satisfactorily completed.

- Tracking errors: The leader either actively monitors deviations from standards or waits for errors to occur and then takes action.

## Transformational Leadership

- Motivating or inspiring people: Leaders behave in ways that foster team spirit. They get people involved. People identify with them. They are charismatic.

- Stimulating the intellect: The leader stimulates innovation and creativity by questioning assumptions and reframing the problem in ways that help lead to solutions (note link to double-loop learning).

- Indicating individualized consideration: Leaders respect differences between people. They delegate responsibility.

According to Bass & Avolio's research, every leader displays each style to some extent. No leader exhibits solely transactional behaviors; none show only transformational behaviors; none are completely laissez-faire. The difference lies in the extent to which these behaviors are employed, which in turn determines the leader's effectiveness. The most effective leaders they studied predominantly used transformational behaviors, less often transactional behaviors, and very rarely showed a laissez-faire indifference. Conversely the most ineffective leaders tended towards inactivity, exhibiting mainly laissez faire and least frequently the transformational styles. Moderately effective leaders were in the middle, using primarily transactional behaviors and to much lesser extent, transformation or laissez-faire.

Bass & Avolio have done a great deal of empirical research to support their contentions that:

  a) The range of behaviors they have identified are valid dimensions to measure

b) Leaders who are considered more effective use much more transformational-type behaviors than transactional. Conversely, less effective leaders use far more of the transactional and less of the transformational.

There are obvious similarities between Bass & Avolio's work and that of Blake & Mouton's Managerial Grid. There is also some overlap with single- and double-loop learning theories. Whether Bass & Avolio's bipolar approach that traces a continuum from transactional to transformational is more useful than the Managerial Grid is open to debate. The message, however, seems to be the same: leaders who are able to overcome defensiveness to create an open environment where feedback and learning work hand-in-hand are better able to engage all employees in accomplishing the work of the organization... and thus better able to create transformational change.

Another interesting view that may straddle both schools of thought is one proposed by Howard Gardner, who, in the late twentieth century, propounded theories relating to multiple intelligences (an idea since popularized by Daniel Goleman in his best-selling books on "Emotional Intelligence"). In *Leading Minds: Anatomy of Leadership*, Gardner examines 11 individuals "who, by word and/or personal example, markedly influenced ... the behaviors, thoughts, and/or feelings of a significant number of their fellow human beings." These individuals included Alfred P. Sloan, Jr. (who led General Motors through its formative years and developed a management model that set an example emulated by countless other organizations in the 20th century), Martin Luther King Jr.,

Margaret Thatcher, General George C. Marshall, and Albert Einstein.

Gardner's major finding was that all 11 leaders had an unmistakable "authenticity," a word also used to describe 9,9 team-oriented leaders. Gardner writes, "Leaders such as Marshall convey their stories by the kinds of lives they themselves lead and, through example, seek to inspire in their followers."

James Collins (co-author of *Built to Last*) took a similar approach, except he focused on the factors that allow good companies to sustain "great" results. In a monumental study of 1435 companies, he and his team identified 11 that met the "good to great" criteria (summarized in the aptly named sequel, *Good to Great*). As part of this work, Collins identified five levels of leadership:

**Level 1: Highly Capable Individual**—Makes productive contributions at an individual level; has good knowledge, skills and work habits.

**Level 2: Contributing Team Member**—Contributes individual capabilities to the achievement of group objectives and works effectively with others in a group setting.

**Level 3: Competent Manager**—Organizes people and resources toward the effective and efficient pursuit of pre-determined objectives.

**Level 4: Effective Leader**—Catalyzes commitment to and vigorous pursuit of a clear and compelling vision, stimulating higher performance standards.

**Level 5: Executive**—Builds enduring greatness through a paradoxical blend of personal humility and professional will.

One factor that distinguished the 11 great companies from all the others was having a CEO who displayed Level 5 Leadership:

> *"The good-to-great executives were all cut from the same cloth. It didn't matter whether the company was consumer or industrial, in crisis or steady state, offered services or products. It didn't matter when the transition took place or how big the company. All the good-to-great companies had Level 5 leadership at the time of transition. Furthermore, the absence of Level 5 leadership showed up as a consistent pattern in the comparison companies [that were unable to sustain their success]."*

If you read Collins' book, you'll see that Level 5 leadership equates closely to the 9,9 Grid style and the Transformational leader. All three of these approaches emphasize learning over defensiveness, a blend of both people-concern and production-concern, and credibility gained by demonstrating behaviors consistent with espoused theories.

# Prescriptive vs. Learning Models of Leadership

The main limitation of most classic theories of leadership is that they are **rational** models that try to **prescribe** exactly what a leader should be. People go out and observe others they consider to be effective leaders, then come up with a list of characteristics or capabilities that define those leaders. What these models fail to take into account is that leadership is contextual, and that the combination of various leadership styles and personality traits leads to infinite variations of "effective leadership" in practice.

Fortunately, there's a secret we've learned that may sound surprising: You don't need to resolve the debate about whether leaders are born or made, or come up with a list of leadership "competencies" in order to improve leadership in your organization. No matter how you got to where you are—whether from learned skills or inherited abilities—you can become a more effective leader by developing a deep understanding of true 9,9 Team Leadership, and opening yourself to double-loop learning. This is a **dynamic** model of how to improve leadership based on learning.

We're not saying that an approach based on modeling "leadership" is worthless. In fact, many excellent leaders will tell you that they learned a lot by observing and emulating the skills and behaviors of other leaders. But they'll also tell you they weren't simply trying to create a checklist of skills they had to master. Rather, they learned from these leaders while at the same time striving to be true to themselves and their uniqueness as human beings responsible for leading others— thus making their learning dynamic (and, as Gardner would state, creating *authentic leadership*).

## Chapter 3 Summary

- Traditionally, leadership models have taken a prescriptive approach, defining a list of traits or characteristics that are required for effective leadership.

- In studying these models, you'll find that effective leadership is described in ways consistent with 9,9 Team Leadership based on Model II assumptions and double-loop learning.

- The models are instructive about behaviors that help leaders be effective.

- Whether or not you subscribe to one of these other models, you can improve your own skills by practicing double-loop learning.

# 4

# The Struggle to Be
# a True Team Leader

THE PATHWAY to becoming a more effective leader may be starting to look deceptively simple. All you need to do is get some feedback to become a double-loop learner and work towards a 9,9 leadership style, right? Unfortunately, experience shows that both these goals are much harder to achieve than they sound, as we'll explore below.

## Challenge #1: Double-Loop Learning

*Carl was a very caring but over-protective CEO. He became convinced, based on the advice of well-informed outsiders, that the cause of his company's inability to innovate was the culture of dependency that had evolved over time, partly attributable to his Paternalistic behavior. Analysis had shown that the company consistently promoted managers who stifled the creativity of those working for them. The managers were well-intentioned, but did not delegate enough authority to their subordinates.*

> *Carl decided to change things. He orga-*
> *nized several meetings, brought in consultants,*
> *and launched a program to change the culture*
> *of the organization. When the program had been*
> *underway for several months, a junior member of*
> *the organization mentioned to Carl that she had*
> *encountered just the kinds of behaviors that he*
> *wanted to eradicate. Carl empathized immedi-*
> *ately: "Julie, if you encounter the kinds of behaviors*
> *we are trying to get rid of, I want you to understand*
> *that I have an open door policy. Give me a call, and*
> *I will ensure the proper action is taken to ensure our*
> *change initiative is successful." Julie walked away*
> *with a spring in her step, energized by Carl's com-*
> *ments and strong show of support.*

Take a closer look at what Carl has just accomplished. In one breath he said, "I want you all to behave as adults, to share control, to contribute more meaningfully to this company's performance." Yet in the next breath he said, "Julie, I will solve your problems for you; just give me a call. I will use my power and authority to deal with those controlling executives that are blocking your progress." He is doing exactly what he is accusing his senior-level subordinates of doing!

Though his intention was to get more people involved in the organization, Carl's actions had the opposite effect. He took control of the situation and suggested a solution that ran completely counter to his intentions. Imagine if Carl repeatedly carried out on the promise he made to Julie. Over time everyone reporting to him would learn to submit to his mandates to "behave as I tell you to behave," and would never develop their own skills in resolving conflict and changing behavior.

This kind of thinking and the actions that flow from it are commonplace. It causes dissent to go underground and fester, undermining the progress of the change that is so urgently sought.

Such self-deception illustrates the first hurdle we all face in the quest to become double-loop learners: Like Carl, we unintentionally act in ways that are self-defeating because we are in a state of "not knowing what we don't know."

Before offering a solution, let's take Carl's situation one step further. A colleague pointed out to Carl the fundamental flaw in his approach and Carl agreed that his reaction to Julie had been wrong. He then faced the most critical steps for any leader wanting to improve: figuring out how to recognize when his behavior is part of the problem, and developing more constructive behaviors.

For example, after his experience with Julie, Carl thought he had learned that he should not rescue an employee. Yet here's what happened at a later meeting, this time with a vice president: The VP told Carl he was nervous about an upcoming presentation to the Board, so Carl said he would handle it in order to save the VP from all that stress. In short, Carl to the rescue, once again!

Don't be too harsh in judging Carl; if you've ever tried to change one of your own behavior patterns, you'll sympathize with his predicament. For one thing, most of us are blind to our own style of management. We judge ourselves on our intentions not on our actions. For another, it is difficult to generalize from one situation to the next. (Until it was again pointed out to him, Carl simply didn't realize he was "rescuing" the VP.) Lastly, it is incredibly easy to slip into established behavior patterns without realizing it.

In short, the kind of self-discovery and invention needed to become a true Team Leader is much harder than it may sound.

## *Learning About Our Behavior*

The challenges we face in learning about our behavior are the same challenges fundamental to ALL learning (see Figure 11):

### Figure 11: Four Steps of Learning

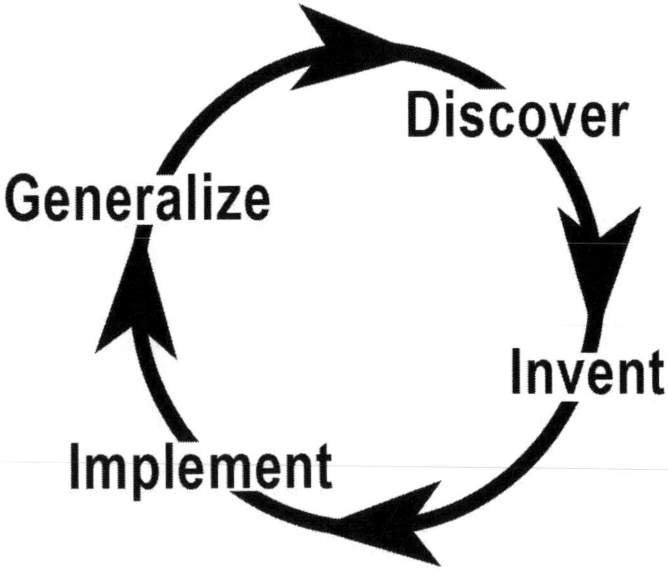

1. **Discover** we have a problem.

2. **Invent** a solution.

3. **Implement** the solution.

4. **Generalize** the solution.

Though these steps sound simple, carrying them out is hard.

- As individuals we are often blind to the problems we face and unaware of how we ourselves may be contributing to a problem. Because we can't **discover** the real problem, we address symptoms and end up repeating the same counterproductive behavior over and over again.

- Even once we know we have a problem, if all we do is act based on Model I assumptions, we will simply continue to skate along the surface because we'll be unable to **invent** a way to alter the problem behavior at its fundamental level.

- Even if we are able to figure out (invent) a solution, we will often find we cannot **implement** it (and if we do implement it, the challenge is sustaining it). It's easy to slip into our old, familiar ways without realizing it.

- After working our way through steps 1 to 3, we may have solved a particular problem in a particular situation, but it can still be difficult to **generalize** to other problems in other situations. In Carl's case, for example, he had not understood the general principle involved and therefore was unable to avoid repeating the controlling behavior in different circumstances.

Applying the learning steps to our behavior—turning the magnifying glass inward—is never easy. But Argyris's theories about double-loop learning provide more clues on how we can make it happen. People operating in a Model II mode assume they don't have all the answers. They are therefore open to receiving input, particularly on how their own behavior affects the achievement or non-achievement of the desired results.

## *The Catch-22 of double-loop learning*

Unfortunately, double-loop learning is something of a Catch-22, a problem you can't solve unless you already have the solution! According to Argyris, a double-loop learner has to master *all* of these steps before mastering *any* of them. As we saw, Carl had difficulty learning how to discover when he was behaving in a counterproductive manner. It was pointed out to him after his interaction with one subordinate (Julie), but then he didn't realize he was doing the very same thing with his Vice President.

As Argyris explains, Carl's inability to discover is easily explained: he needs to be able to use all four learning steps (discover, invent, implement, generalize) just to discover he has a problem. He outlines it this way (Table 1):

### Table 1: Learning Steps for Discovery

| 1 DISCOVER inconsistencies: Recognize what you want to have happen (espoused theories) is different from what is happening (theories-in-use) | 2 Discover that you do not know **how to discover** what you want to discover | 3 **Invent** how to discover | 4 **Implement** behavior needed for discovery | 5 **Generalize** about effective discovery processes |
|---|---|---|---|---|

*Argyris's insight: You need all the learning steps to do Discovery well.*

This pattern continues for all the learning steps, which produces the "double loop" in double-loop learning (see Figure 12).

## Figure 12: Double-loop Learning

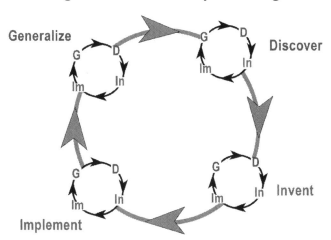

In our example, Carl did not reject the idea that he might be part of the problem. He became aware—discovered—that there was an inconsistency in one particular circumstance. But the next time he was faced with a situation in which he was acting counterproductively (this time with the VP), he was still blind to the adverse impact of his long-entrenched behavior patterns. The Catch-22: Carl will continue to struggle with knowing when he's creating a problem until he has learned how to "Discover, Invent, Implement, and Generalize" how to "discover."

Yet despite the challenge, creating a feedback–rich environment in which individuals are non-defensive to the feedback of others can facilitate double loop learning. In this kind of setting, many leaders have learned how to break out of this Catch-22—and it's not as difficult as it may sound at first.

The secret has been discussed several times already: as individuals, we usually can't see our own problems... but others have much better eyesight! By opening ourselves to seeing ourselves as others see us, we are in a better position to use all of the learning steps.

When individuals operate in a single-loop learning mode they will tend to repeatedly make the same mistake. If, however, they have learned to be non-defensive, they will be open to having others point out their anti-learning behavior. This allows them to become much more aware of situations in which they are likely to operate in a rigid single-loop learning mode and will eventually gain the double-loop learning skills.

Here's an example:

> *Tony, a senior executive in a manufacturing company, has a very hard-driving management style. He finds it difficult to deal with individuals who do not share his sense of urgency, especially in areas that he considers very important to the company. Yet he and his colleagues have explored leadership concepts and have collaborated in creating a climate where they assist each other in overcoming their Model I assumptions and behaviors. In fact, Tony had encouraged his peers to point out to him when he unthinkingly took control of a situation in a way that shut down productive problem-solving.*
>
> *At a routine staff meeting, James, the IT manager, said that a serious Internet security issue had not been resolved, the third time in as many*

*meetings that Internet security had come to the fore. James' strong suit is not communication, but he began haltingly to explain the status of the issue. Tony's impatience at the perceived delays caused him to seize control of the situation. He told James to bring his entire IT group to a meeting later that day and dictated a number of steps he would like James to take to prepare for the meeting. James fell silent.*

*Despite his good intentions, Tony was completely unaware of the controlling manner he employed. After the meeting Brian pointed out to Tony that his behavior was counterproductive. As it turned out James had dealt with the issue. A completely new software program had been purchased, and factors beyond James' control (the software had to be modified to fit their company's system) had delayed implementation of the solution. Thus Tony's total lack of inquiry in this instance created duplication of effort.*

*Brian pointed out to Tony that James operates three management levels below him and was completely cowed by Tony's manner (the fact that Tony has a reputation for tearing people apart in meetings did not help in this instance). James decided that keeping his head down was the best policy—a Model I, single-loop learning response on James's part. As Brian talked, Tony's initial reaction was one of surprise. He started to defend his actions in the meeting... but then caught himself and recollected a similar situation (nothing to do with IT, that's why he did not make the connection himself). He acknowledged to himself it was exactly the same pattern of behavior, and thanked Brian for bringing*

> *the matter to his attention. He then immediately*
> *made his way to James' office to rectify the situation.*

There are obviously times when a leader must take decisive action. However, in this situation Tony used his seniority (power and authority) to completely take control of a situation, shutting James down in the process. Tony's deeply ingrained Model I assumptions led him to jump to conclusions (without validating them) and take unilateral actions. If he and his colleagues had not established a ground rule that it's OK for them to catch each other employing counterproductive behaviors, Tony would most likely have continued his pattern of behavior. Instead, because he got the chance to see his behavior through others' eyes, he was able to start the learning process…and, over time, learn how to monitor and adjust his behavior before it became a problem.

One of Tony's biggest challenges—which we saw with Carl, and is true for all of us—is learning to *generalize*. Though Tony had encountered his Model I methods in one situation, the fact that he had not employed them in an IT-related problem made it difficult for him to make the connections.

Having an environment where others are not afraid to point out our behaviors is a huge step forward in the process of learning how to generalize. Working with others who are struggling with similar dilemmas can be effective in slowly untying the knots that prevent true learning and effective problem solving. Our blind spots are usually evident to others. If we work in an environment that encourages the candid giving and receiving of personal feedback (face to face), and we ourselves are non-defensive when receiving feedback, we can gradually get better at each stage of double-loop learning. Others can help us discover problems that we are unaware of, we can draw on their creativity to help us invent solutions, and so on.

## Challenge #2:
## Striving Towards the 9,9 Ideal

*Bill was in charge of a large bureaucratic department. He had undergone in-depth Grid training and though highly motivated to introduce these approaches in his department, it took some years before he could pull it off. Eventually, though, he organized a workshop which proved to be very successful. The people working for Bill responded very positively to the idea that open, candid feedback would become part and parcel of the way in which they would work together in the future.*

*In the course of preparing, delivering, and following up on the workshop, the instructor, John, learned that Bill had a strong commitment to the 9,9 style of management and believed that he was very much a 9,9 leader himself. However, it also became evident that Bill's subordinates viewed him as a 9+9 Paternal leader. The examples of Bill's behaviors that his subordinates described to John made it clear that Bill's image of himself did not at all mirror reality and that his self-deception was the cause of significant problems within the department.*

*John decided to discuss this matter with Bill. He began to carefully explore the fact that*

*Bill's view of his behavior was not shared by his subordinates. As it turned out, Bill became very defensive. Further attempts to have him listen to his subordinates proved futile. Bill discontinued the organizational development activities that he had initiated and, from accounts some time later, the department continued to operate under Bill's paternalistic, overly controlling leadership.*

Bill's story is in no way unique. From our personal experiences as well observations of hundreds of leaders, it's clear that changing behavior isn't easy even once someone knows there is a better way. It's hard work and not everyone succeeds. We tell this story not to discourage you from trying, but rather to help you set realistic expectations around change. You have to really be open to hearing feedback if you want to become a 9,9 Leader. And even if you are, don't expect change to happen overnight; remember that you're trying to change your ingrained behaviors. Initially, you'll have to be very deliberate and self-conscious about trying out new behaviors. If you try to do too much too fast, you won't succeed. Go slowly. And don't expect perfection.

The discussions so far lead us naturally into the next section where we'll examine a well known model that graphically shows how, over time, with the right interpersonal strategies, a leader can develop much greater self-awareness and an orientation of continuous learning.

## Chapter 4 Summary

• Becoming a 9,9 team leader is more difficult than it may sound at first.

• Being aware of effective leadership behaviors is a prerequisite for improvement, but it's very difficult for anyone to consistently act in 9,9 ways even when they are aware of the ideals.

• We need to be skilled in all the steps of double-loop learning before we can practice any individual step most effectively.

• However, just being open to honest feedback can help us overcome the barriers to double-loop learning.

# 5

# Creating a Feedback- Friendly Environment

*A new dot.com was formed by a number of Ph.D. computer whizzes who were very savvy technically, but who had little formal knowledge of or interest in "behavior." Take Tim, for instance. He was young, ambitious, taught by a demanding father to work hard and expect nothing less from others. He not only had a conceit common to the intelligent—that he was smart enough to make decisions on his own—but also believed it was his job as a leader to make decisions to pass on to his staff. His natural tendency to focus on business was exacerbated by working in a new company: he had no patience for what he considered chatter while on the job, neither sharing much about himself nor inquiring about others.*

THE REALITY of corporate life—and life in general—is that work is accomplished through the interactions of groups of people, not by individuals (that's why "effective interaction" is the key third circle in the model introduced in the Preface). This presents an interesting challenge for leaders: they have the choice of behaving in ways that increase their awareness of themselves and others, or in ways that create distance between them and their fellow team members.

Initially, Tim had chosen the second path, isolating himself from his staff and even his peers to some extent. His behavior discouraged the openness and trust needed to create an environment where honest feedback is not only possible but encouraged. In all likelihood, Tim's behavior reflected what behavior experts describe as a "poor Johari Window." A simple model helpful in thinking about the process of relating to others, the Johari Window relates two factors:

- How much we know about ourselves (self-knowledge)

- How much others know about us (disclosure)

When these two dimensions are put together, you end up with a simple four-quadrant matrix (see Figure 13):

- Knowledge that is known to both you and to others (Public or Open knowledge)

- Knowledge that is known to you but not to others (Private or Hidden knowledge)

- Knowledge that others have about you but that you are unaware of (knowledge to which you are blind)

- Knowledge that neither of you have (unknown knowledge)

## Figure 13: The Johari Window

|  | Known to Self | Not Known to Self |
|---|---|---|
| **Known to Others** | OPEN | BLIND |
| **Not Known to Others** | HIDDEN | UNKNOWN |

In Tim's case, his Johari Window looked like Figure 14: He was a very private person and therefore there was a lot that others did not know about him. He was also ignorant of how his behavior affected others (little self-knowledge).

## Figure 14: Tim's Johari Window
*Tim has little knowledge about himself, and the people around him know little about his working style and preferences, either. This is a poor Johari window.*

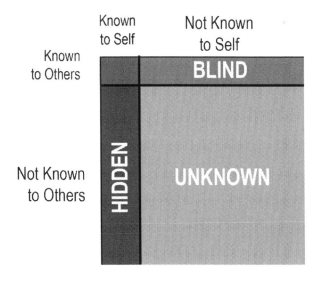

The premise behind the Johari Window is that better communication grows out of people sharing ever-larger areas of knowledge about each other. We can follow two distinct strategies to improve two-way sharing between ourselves and others:

1) **Receiving feedback on our own behavior.** You've read this refrain several times already, and here's yet another reason why being open to feedback is an effective leadership strategy: doing so "opens the window." Listening to how our behavior affects others gives us ideas about what is and isn't working. It also helps us draw on the creativity of others to think about how to do better.

2) **Disclosing information about ourselves**—sharing our thinking, reasoning, and other relevant information with others. Telling people about what we're thinking and why helps them become more involved in decisions that affect them. This in turn creates trust and encourages feedback, which increases effectiveness and satisfaction within a team. Not sharing information is behavior expected from 9,1 power-and-control managers who think they can maintain an advantage only by controlling who knows what. In contrast, a 9,9 team leader has a mindset that the default should be to share information, and only in special circumstances to restrict it. That doesn't mean you need to tell people about everything going on in your business and personal life! Rather, share information that will help:

- Provide a context for an impending business decision (such as budget concerns, revenue expectations, conditions in other parts of your company)

- Create a personal bond ("My daughter is a soccer player, too!")

- Describe personal issues that may affect your job performance ("My mom's in the hospital and I'm having a hard time concentrating")

Together, these two strategies create a larger Public or Open quadrant in the Johari Window (see Figure 15).

## Figure 15: Increasing Public ("Open") Knowledge

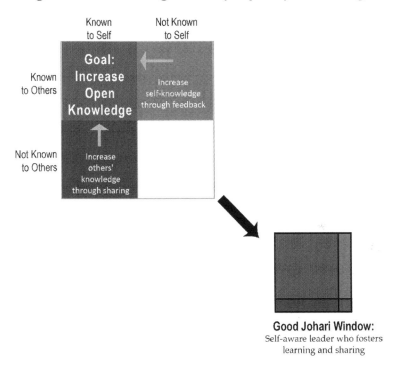

**Good Johari Window:**
Self-aware leader who fosters
learning and sharing

The Johari Window reinforces the perception that one step in becoming more effective as an individual is to understand and improve our connections with others. In doing so, we not only find ways to do better ourselves but also contribute to the effectiveness of those around us.

---

### Chapter 5 Summary

- Historically, few organizations have created environments where feedback to leaders is not only welcome but encouraged.

- Just saying to subordinates that you want feedback will not automatically bring about change.

- Take the initiative by opening your Johari window— sharing relevant information about yourself and decisions you are facing, and drawing out information from others.

---

# Conclusion to Part I

Though Tim, the dot.com co-founder introduced in the previous chapter, didn't share much personal information about himself, he wasn't shy about stating his opinions on business-related issues. He would state and defend his beliefs loudly and frequently to anyone who would listen. One of his favorite targets of complaint was Ken, another co-founder, and what he perceived as Ken's lack of spine. He thought Ken should give more direct orders and not worry so much about how people were feeling.

Unfortunately, there was something that Tim didn't realize: nearly everyone else greatly respected Ken, valued Ken's management style, and thought Ken had more to contribute to the company than did Tim. It wasn't until the management team held a structured feedback session that Tim learned how his attitudes and behavior were producing the exact opposite result from his intentions: he was alienating everyone and making it harder for the company to work effectively.

Since that meeting, Tim has learned to temper his defensive behavior. He still holds strong opinions, but he does a lot more listening and a lot less talking nowadays. His opinions are now subject to change based on what he hears and learns, and he's more focused on having his entire team—all the people around him—succeed. He now freely *admits that his old thinking was wrong, and that he is now more effective both at the office and in his personal life. (In fact, the whole management team learned a lot from the feedback sessions and its members have become far more effective leaders for this company.)*

As Tim's story illustrates, the ability to link strategy to execution through effective interaction—which is the basis for Three Circle Model described in the Preface—has to start with individual skills. To become 9,9 leaders, we must overcome the natural defensiveness that causes us to act in non-productive, Model I ways. Once defensiveness starts to subside, we can begin the journey towards becoming skilled double-loop learners, constantly improving our effectiveness. And from there, we will have a solid base upon which to build effective interactions with others.

Tim is typical of the success stories we've seen when people receive training and follow-up coaching on improving their own leadership skills. Regardless of individual personality types—from quiet introverted individuals to highly assertive extroverts—most people are doing the best they can with the tools and information they have. Unfortunately, if they operate in a vacuum, they're likely to be satisfied with their performance, unaware of how much more they could achieve. Fortunately, once they get over the initial shock of hearing honest feedback about their behaviors, their natural motivation to contribute to the organization and their respect for their coworkers leads to some remarkable transformations.

What Tim's example also teaches us is that trying to improve our individual skills in isolation from what is going on around us is an impossibility. Self-awareness and a desire to improve as an individual is critical to becoming a more effective leader, but we need to work with the people around us, not only to get better ourselves but to improve everyone's effectiveness. And that's what we'll explore in Part II.

# PART II

# Team & Organizational Effectiveness

# Part II Introduction

*At a workshop a few years ago, Randy learned that he was a strong 9,1 task-oriented leader. He also learned how that affected the people around him. The lessons sank in, but he found it difficult to adopt 9,9 team leadership behaviors. At first he was just going through the motions, asking his direct reports for their opinions and perceptions and listening to their concerns. With the help of a mentor, he stuck with this new plan for about 6 months. He then told his mentor that frankly he didn't see any changes around him, and wondered if all the effort was worth it.*

*Before giving up, however, Randy was convinced by his mentor to simply ask people what the impact had been of his change in attitude. He was floored by what he heard. His direct reports all said he was much more approachable, and they felt more comfortable bringing problems to him... problems they subsequently solved because they could benefit from Randy's expertise. All of them believed they were far more productive now. After that meeting, Randy was no longer just going through the motions. He became more committed to understanding what 9,9 team leadership was all about and how he could practice it more fully.*

Randy's study demonstrates an important facet of leadership: his *individual* strengths and limitations had a profound impact on the effectiveness of his work groups. Randy's shift to being more open to people led to greater openness and productivity among his work team. Here's a similar situation:

> Susan really identified with the values embodied in the Grid and other "enlightened" management approaches. A sincere, well-meaning person, Susan is, however, also rather defensive. When caught up in a conflict with other managers, her strategy is to challenge people to do the "right thing" for the organization. The people who work with Susan find it difficult to put their finger on what bothers them in their interactions with her. After careful consideration, they come to realize that by her constant reference to doing the right thing ("right" in her definition), she is subtly trying to control the values and goals of the organization.

In contrast to Randy's group, the people working *for* Susan usually gave up trying to work *with* her because they couldn't engage her in a frank discussion of problems. If they tried, she'd soon throw out her "we need to do the right thing" statement designed to stop the discussion and have people convert to her way of thinking. Susan's was fundamentally a Model I strategy, based on Model I assumptions such as protecting herself and not trusting others, that led to single-loop learning.

Achieving the vision of the Three Circle Model—having interactions that drive the execution of business strategy—takes more than a sense of personal enlightenment. As

Randy's and Susan's stories illustrate, the transition from individual awareness and behavior to effective teams and organizations is challenging. We have to move beyond a sense of personal enlightenment to shaping group and organizational behaviors in line with our goals.

The following chapters will take you through well-established ideas that explain:

- **The need to manage your sphere of influence:** Each of us forms part of a dynamic system as we interact with others. A leader's job is to create a climate of growth and learning that drives productivity and results by shaping the quality and substance of interactions with his/her bosses, peers, and subordinates.

- **The power of cultural norms:** Team and organizational habits exert a stronger influence over our individual behavior than we would ever have imagined. To create lasting change, we must change these norms.

- **How to shape team or organizational structure** by understanding how diversity on a team is critical to effectiveness and achieving outstanding results.

# 6

# Managing Your Sphere of Influence

*It would surprise most of the executive staff that "schmoozing" didn't come naturally to their CEO, Kathy. On any given day, she'd be lunching with the banker, or meeting a customer, or perhaps talking to the Mayor. She was something of a legend in the company for starting the monthly "Exec breakfasts," informal get-togethers that were initially met with skepticism but turned out to help everyone on the Exec team keep abreast of important developments in the company.*

# # #

*Nathan was proud of his promotion to Supervisor. His worst fear was that he'd mess it up somehow. It didn't take him long to realize that there was a lot he didn't know. But he didn't give up. Instead, he made it a point to talk with the other supervisors and ask for their guidance. He also set up one-on-one meetings with each of the reps for his key suppliers.*

# # #

*Irene was the new President for a large division of a multinational corporation. It didn't take her long to figure out the difference between two of her direct reports, Teri and Jacob. Teri seemed to have nothing but contempt for her counterparts at corporate headquarters. When Teri was involved with anything that required cooperation from corporate headquarters, Irene inevitably had to step in to smooth ruffled feathers. When Jacob was in charge, everything went smoothly. Irene knew for a fact that Jacob had spent time developing personal relationships with a number of people over at corporate.*

To the cynical, it might seem that Nathan, Kathy, and Jacob were playing politics, trying to manipulate people to serve their own purposes. But in fact they were all practicing good leadership. By virtue of their role, leaders are seldom carrying out the daily work of the organization. Instead, their job is to make it possible for their work unit to move down a path to success. They do this by developing a deep understanding of the needs and capabilities of those over whom they have authority or influence, and by understanding how to mold the opinions and decisions of those who have authority or influence over them and their organization. This creates a **sphere of influence** (see Figure 16) that defines a leader's critical environment.

## Figure 16: Sphere of Influence

We each have our own sphere of influence; the higher up we are in the organization, the broader the sphere and the greater the potential impact. For example, an organization's top leaders...

- Have spheres of influence that extend well beyond the organization's boundaries

- Can block progress or open up the opportunities for achieving goals as no other team member can

- Shape how others operate within their own spheres of influence

In fact, it's easy to argue that a leader's primary job is to create the conditions for success of the organization through managing his or her sphere of influence. A leader's ability to achieve desired results is determined by the quality and substance of their interactions with others—what they choose to present to others, what information they seek from others, how they relate to the other groups or individuals, and so on.

Managing your sphere of influence happens in numerous ways. Let's look at two ways in which 9,9 team-oriented leaders proactively manage their spheres of influence.

# 1. Decision Making/Planning

In many organizations, those in positions of power and authority make all the decisions; in others, decisions seem to simply happen, and no one is quite sure how. Leaders who are aware of the need to effectively manage their spheres of influence know that it's important *to decide how to decide*: they use their judgment, experience and maturity to make deliberate decisions about who to involve when in planning and decision making. Broadly speaking, a leader can choose one of four decision-making modes:

- One alone: the leader will take unilateral action
- One on one: the leader will involve someone else in decision-making/planning
- One on some: the leader will involve several others in the decision
- One on all: the leader will involve the entire organization

The basic principle is that if someone or some group is affected by a decision, they should be involved in the decision-making process in some way. This involvement can take many forms:

- Being informed when a decision has been made
- Being asked to provide input/opinions
- Being asked to gather data

- Being asked to evaluate the options
- Being asked to make the decision

Effective decision-making is a prominent feature that distinguishes a 9,9 orientation from other styles because:

- *Commitment* to decisions improves the likelihood of long-term support and effective implementation; compliance is not enough

- With the right management processes, 2+2 can equal more than 4: synergy and creativity bloom when people are involved at appropriate times and in appropriate ways

- People will feel more commitment when their personal goals are aligned with the organization's goals

# 2. Capitalizing on Team Members' Abilities

*Miriam was in charge of a small but high-level work team. She knew from past experience that her strengths lay in creative thinking and visioning; her weakness was a lack of interest in implementation! For her group to be effective, she knew that she had to put people on her team who would either feed her creativity or be able to take responsibility for bringing projects to completion.*

Quite consciously, Miriam was working effectively within her sphere of influence by being deliberate in the skills she sought and encouraged among her team members. Her instincts are supported by scientific research. In the 1970s, Dr. Meredith Belbin (now of Cambridge University) and his team spent nine years studying management teams that were undergoing executive development and working in situations that simulated real world challenges. Every individual involved in the team exercises underwent detailed psychometric and mental ability testing prior to participating in the simulations. Belbin's group amassed a huge amount of data on the relationship between team success, personality factors, mental capabilities and creativity. Their work is unique in that it directly relates specific team member skills to team success.

Belbin's fundamental discovery was that each of us naturally performs one or more specific functions or roles on a team and **that to be highly effective, a team needs a balance of these roles.** (In fact, Belbin could accurately predict which teams would succeed and which would fail based on the mix of roles represented.)

In all, Belbin's research identified nine different roles that capture particular ways in which team members contribute to team success (see Table 2, next page). The roles in which we are most effective, that come most naturally to us, are our preferred roles (most of us have more than one). Each of us can also effectively fill other roles, which Belbin calls manageable, though doing so will result in a certain amount of stress. The roles for which we are not at all suited are what Belbin calls least-preferred; we can be forced into these roles, but will be under a lot of stress and will likely not perform well. Each individual has his or her own mix of preferred, manageable, and least-preferred roles.

## Table 2: Preferred Team Roles

| Role | Team-Role Contribution | Allowable Weaknesses |
|---|---|---|
| Plant | Creative, imaginative, unorthodox. Solves difficult problems. | Ignores details. Too preoccupied to communicate effectively. |
| Resource Investigator | Extroverted, enthusiastic, communicative. Explores opportunities. Develops contacts. | Overoptimistic. Loses interest once initial enthusiasm has passed. |
| Coordinator | Mature, confident, a good chairperson. Clarifies goals, promotes decision-making, delegates well. | Can be seen as manipulative. Delegates personal work. |
| Shaper | Challenging, dynamic, thrives on pressure. Has the drive and courage to overcome obstacles. | Can provoke others. Hurts people's feelings. |
| Monitor / Evaluator | Sober, strategic and discerning. Sees all options. Judges accurately. | Lacks drive and ability to inspire others. Overly critical. |
| Team Worker | Cooperative, mild, perceptive and diplomatic. Listens, builds, averts friction, calms the waters. | Indecisive in crunch situations. Can be easily influenced. |
| Implementer | Disciplined, reliable, conservative and efficient. Turns ideas into practical actions. | Somewhat inflexible. Slow to respond to new possibilities. |
| Completer / Finisher | Painstaking, conscientious. Searches out errors and omissions.Delivers on time. | Inclined to worry unduly. Anxious. Reluctant to delegate. Can be a nit-picker. |
| Specialist | Single-minded, self-starting, dedicated. Provides knowledge and skills in rare supply. | Contributes only on a narrow front. Dwells on technicalities. Overlooks the big picture. |

Significantly, Belbin also discovered that the personal attributes that create a given strength generally come with specific deficiencies or allowable weaknesses. The two are a package: you can't get the strength without also getting the weakness. Effective teams recognize this fact and deliberately mold their membership to create a good balance. Someone who is a natural Plant will never be good at details; someone who excels as a Team Worker may not be decisive enough to be the team leader.

Belbin's research has very practical applications for leaders who want to shape effective work teams. He identified specific combinations that were predictive of team effectiveness or ineffectiveness:

### Factors contributing to ineffective teams

1) No Monitor Evaluators: the team is unlikely to carefully weigh options when making decisions.

2) Too many Monitor Evaluators: paralysis-from-analysis outweighs creative ability.

3) No Completer/Finishers and Implementers: the team will create good strategies but not follow through.

### Factors contributing to effective teams

4) Including a Plant on the team will lead to more ideas and better strategies, but will also require Monitor/Evaluators and Coordinators.

5) Resource Investigators provide an external orientation.

6) Shapers will recognize the need for urgency which will have a significant impact on results, essential to high-performance teams.

7) Having too many Shapers leads to excessive conflict. Make certain there is a Team Worker to facilitate relationships.

8) Have a Specialist in situations where specialized knowledge is required.

Teams that do not have a balance of roles or a plan to address deficiencies can be predicted to fail. But this does not mean that every team needs to have nine members, each person representing a single role. As noted, people tend to be strong in a number of roles, and the key is to make sure there is a proper mix of roles represented on the team.

In short, to best shape the teams around them (both those on which they participate and those they manage), a leader should:

- Understand each person's Preferred Team Roles—the roles in which that person has aptitude and learned skills

- Carefully structure teams to achieve a good balance of roles

- Deliberately exploit the different strengths of those on the team and compensate for weaknesses

## Determining Preferred Roles

The process of evaluating team strengths and weaknesses has been made practical and inexpensive by software that automates the process. Using that software, you can...

- Determine an individual's "preferred role," as perceived both the team member and his/her cohorts

- Evaluate team dynamics, suggesting who should fill which role

Understanding preferred roles is an eye-opener for most people! They are able at last to understand why previous teams succeeded or failed. They learn their own preferred roles, and the strengths and weaknesses that go with the roles. There is a sense of liberation in realizing that they have weaknesses because they have strengths, and that these weaknesses are OK *as long as they are managed.*

This principle applies to all sorts of teams, from project teams to work groups. Miriam, the executive described above, applied this knowledge to help her better manage her sphere of influence by deliberately creating balance between strengths and "allowable weakness" on her management team.

## The Oiled Cog

We all know that what distinguishes a leader—formal or informal—is power and authority. Their actions and decisions have a much wider impact than those of others in the organization. That's why an effective 9,9 leader is like an oiled cog at the center of a complex mechanism, helping the organization's work progress smoothly and efficiently. Conversely, an ineffective leader is like a rusty cog, impeding progress at every turn.

Previous chapters in this book have provided clues on how to make sure you're not a rusty cog: being aware of your own leadership tendencies, working to reduce defensiveness, becoming a double-loop learner, and opening your Johari Window. The new piece of the puzzle here is that leaders have to be cognizant of their spheres of influence and make deliberate choices about how to interact within those spheres in order to be most effective.

### Chapter 6 Summary

- Each of us has people whom we can influence due either to our organizational position and/or relationships we have developed (our sphere of influence).

- The most effective leaders consciously manage their spheres by (a) taking the initiative to develop relationships with those who fall within their spheres, (b) making appropriate choices around involving others in decision making, and (c) consciously selecting team members based on their Preferred Roles to make sure the team as a whole has an effective combination of skills and weaknesses.

# 7

# The Strong, Silent Hand that Shapes Behavior

IN THEIR book, *Productivity: the Human Side*, Blake and Mouton relate the following story:

> Of the 10 plants operated by one chemical company, nine had exemplary safety records. The tenth was another story: safety was a joke. For nearly a decade, the company tried everything it could to improve safety at that plant. Management spoke about safety every chance they could, they emphasized the poor record at this plant. But nothing changed. They fired all the supervisors. Still nothing changed. They fired the supervisors of the supervisors. No change.
>
> Then finally they brought in some behavioral experts who divided the plant employees into small teams. Each team was asked the following question, "We have a bad safety record. What may be the causes and what can we do about it?" After considerable venting and externalizing ("it's not our fault!"), one by one each team reached the point where they admitted, "we may be part of the problem." The teams started brainstorming things

> *that they as a team and as individuals could do to improve safety. Within a year, that plant had the highest safety record in the company, a record it has maintained to this day.*

So far in this book, we've explored ways in which you can affect your own personal behavior, and become aware of how you affect those around you. The next steps in becoming an effective leader are:

1) Understanding how behavior evolves at a group or organizational level

2) Understanding how to influence group behavior.

In short, if you want to get better results from people, it helps to understand how their behaviors are formed. How did the company in Blake and Mouton's story change organizational behavior? By using a 9,9 strategy of exposing the standard or accepted behaviors—the **norms**—so everyone could acknowledge and deal with those that were preventing progress. Norms are patterns of behavior at the group or organizational level that are driven by largely unseen forces. (An individual has habits; organizations have norms.) The impact of norms on behavior is so huge that they are often called the "strong, silent hand" driving the organization.

Few of us would describe our behaviors as following a norm, partly because we're unaware that our actions are subtly influenced over time, and partly because we don't like to think that we're just following the pack. Yet it does happen, and, by understanding norms and how they develop at the team (or group) and organizational levels, we can:

- Appreciate the effort it will take to accomplish widespread behavioral change in the organization

- Target current norms that are impeding effectiveness

## Understanding Organizational Habits

Every group—be it a new team of 3 people or an established company of 3,000—has certain traditions, precedents and past practices that shape acceptable behavior: its norms. These are unwritten rules that people adhere to almost subconsciously; any violation makes them uncomfortable. Think about a group or team you've been on, for example. What were your standard practices around:

- **How decisions were made?** Directed by the boss, majority rule, flip of a coin, consensus, or thrashed so much that no decision ever got made?

- **How conflict was handled?** Suppressed, avoided by trying to please everyone, smoothed over, or ignored until it erupted?

- **How goals were set and communicated?** Were they clearly understood by everyone on the team; was there team agreement on what the goals were; were they imposed by the boss?

- **How meetings were handled?** Did people arrive on time? 15 minutes late? Did people come to contribute or just to listen?

Broaden your scope a little, and you'll find that you're really looking at an organization's behavior system or **culture**, which affects how your team and every person and group in the organization behaves (see Table 3, next two pages).

Of all these practices shaped by the culture, you can learn the most about a culture by studying two them: how power and authority are exercised, and how conflict is resolved. Third most telling is the organization's heroes, it's folklore!

The key to evaluating norms is to assess whether they are productive or counterproductive for your team and your organization. For example, an older computer company became enamored of teamwork some years ago. Everyone in the company had extensive team training, and the new CEO (most likely a Paternal leader in terms of the Managerial Grid) introduced a team-oriented culture. But a few years later, the new norms around teamwork and inclusion were proving disastrous. Nothing could get done without involving nearly everyone, and productivity was down significantly. (In Grid terms, you might say they had drifted towards a Country Club atmosphere—a lot of concern for people and little concern for production.) It would take months to get a project up and running. What started out as a well-intentioned effort to involve employees more in their jobs and the workplace deteriorated into norms that hurt effectiveness and productivity.

# Table 3: Typical Areas of Organizational Norms

**Planning:** Top down? Are ideas shared? Bounced back and forth throughout the organization? Do people negotiate and talk about goals realistically?

**Power and authority,** in terms of...
> **Conflict Resolution:** Are differences openly discussed? Do people argue over real business issues, or about differences in personality or approach? Does a surface politeness cover underlying disagreements?
> **Decision Making:** Is there discussion? Do people strive for consensus? Resort to majority voting?

**Group Collaboration:** How is conflict handled? Do groups talk with each other? Try to undermine each other's work? Operate as independent silos, merely tossing salvos at the other?

**Top-down Communications** (quality and frequency): In more productive companies, bosses are highly visible and often delivers his/her message in person.

**Principles:** Strong companies often have highly motivating underlying principles. A century-old pharmaceutical company has long fostered an attitude of serving the health of the public.

**Folklore:** Who are heroes within the organization? What did they do to attain hero status? Work long hours? Single handedly save an account? Bring people together?

**Status Groups:** The groups within an organization that have the highest status are often reflective of that organization's business drivers. At one market-driven company, marketing people had all the top jobs, the highest salaries, the biggest departments, etc.

**Time at work:** Are people punctual? Habitually early or late? One highly effective company had a norm that people would take long working lunches. When an employee of that company went to a different company, he soon learned that long lunches were unacceptable: people were to take 1/2 hour lunches, no more, no less. He had been ruled by the silent hand!

## Table 3: Typical Areas of Organizational Norms, cont.

**Safety:** Imagine walking into an ordinary meeting room and having the meeting leader tell everyone to locate the nearest fire exit, clear any chairs from exit pathways, look for broken or wobbly legs on the chairs, etc. Sound extreme? Not if you worked at a copper smelting plant where safety is considered critical to making sure people go home alive and well at the end of the day. In that environment, safety wasn't something people could pay attention to now and then; it had to become a routine part of everyday thinking on the job.

**Dress code:** At many high-tech and dot.com companies, the uniform is blue jeans. Wear a suit and you'll feel out of place. The reverse is true on Wall Street.

**The Boss as God:** You may have run into an organization where the CEO simply has to tell his or her secretary to "organize a meeting... now"—and everyone is expected to drop what they are doing to attend. It's very disruptive. At one company where this norm was established, the CEO eventually left. But the new CEO decided he liked that way of doing things. After all, wasn't his time more precious than that of others?

**Overtime:** It's well known that if you join a particular telecommunications firm, you stand a higher than normal chance of having a divorce because you're expected to put in 80 hours a week or more. Nights and weekends are no longer yours to control. While most of us could consider this unreasonable, the company doesn't ambush people with the expectation. It is clearly established before you're hired.

# How Norms Develop

Imagine that you are starting a new widget production line. You hire 10 people and have them work for 20 minutes, then count how many widgets each person made. At first, you'll see a lot of variation: one person will have done 15 widgets, and another just 5. You show everyone the results, then ask people to work for another 20 minutes. You count and publish the results, and run the line a third time, then continue this cycle. What you'll see over time is that everyone's production level will converge on some number, perhaps 9 or 10 widgets. Without ever openly talking about it, your group will have created its own norm to which most people in the group will conform.

Intuitively, we all know that this happens. You work for a company where people start meetings exactly on time, then move to another company where meetings habitually start late. Pretty soon, you'll be a latecomer to meetings as well.

Given the ease and rapidity with which norms develop in an organization, it is important for an executive to understand the key factors that influence their creation: **convergence**, **conformity**, and **cohesion**.

## *Convergence*

Robert Blake and Jane Srygley Mouton, whose work on the Managerial Grid we explored earlier, were renowned for basic behavioral science work that demonstrated how convergence and cohesion drive uniformity of behavior in a group setting. In fact, the widget process above is based on a case cited by Blake & Mouton. In the actual experiment, several test subjects were brought into a darkened room and asked to stare at a pinpoint of light. Though the light is stationary, everyone thinks it's moving (you may have experienced the same phenomenon when staring at stars in a night sky). Each subject is asked to say how much they thought the light moved. Initially, the range of answers is substantial: one person might describe it as moving a few inches, another might see it as moving a few feet.

The experiment continues as the light is flashed on and off in fairly quick succession. In between, participants again state their perceptions of how much the light moved. Within just a few trials, the amount of movement experienced by the individuals converges on a single number (about a foot). Every time you repeat this experiment, the results is exactly the same: though initial estimates vary widely, participants quickly converge on a single answer.

This phenomenon occurs whenever people in a group react to a novel experience. Although personal reactions vary widely at first, those reactions tend to come together—that is, to converge—as the communal experience continues. The same thing happens in a social setting. Attitudes, opinions and feelings in a group tend to converge, forming group norms.

There were two other lessons from the experiments cited by Blake & Mouton:

- **Convergence is invisible to those experiencing it:** A neutral experimenter, unknown to the participants, interviewed them individually after the experiment. Invariably the participants claimed the rest of the group did not influence them. In fact, people denied with increasing conviction that others had any influence on them. Judgments are experienced as strictly personal. From such interviews we can infer that people generally fail to recognize the extent to which their attitudes, opinions, feelings, and actions are influenced by other people. The influence of norms on personal attitudes is by this time firm, but people cannot see it.

- **Norms are persistent:** When participants are brought back to repeat the experiment individually, rather than as part of a group, they invariably estimate the movement of the light very close to the norm established the first time around. This demonstrates that once convergence occurs it has a persistent influence on how people react to future experiences of the same kind.

Simple though it is, this experiment clarified how convergence factors into organizational life. It explained how people tend to shift their attitudes, opinions, feelings, and actions toward a common denominator. When we realize how significant norms are in organizations, we also realize that convergence around those norms can impact productivity: If an individual works in a team that defines and expects high performance, he or she, much like the other team members, will move towards those standards. The reverse is also true: if the team doesn't have high performance standards then the individuals on the team will perform at a much lower level.

Convergence often appears to occur in a spontaneous and natural way. But what are the conditions that encourage convergence and the formation of norms? An understanding of conformity and cohesion provides clues.

## *Conformity and Cohesion*

In a second experiment cited by Blake and Mouton, seven people in a group read the "case of Johnny Rocco," a story that describes the decisions a school system faces in dealing with a young boy about to enter high school who has acted badly. Should Johnny be given love or punishment, and to what degree?

As the seven people begin to discuss the issue, they soon find themselves in approximate agreement. Because of the way the case is written, people will generally agree that love is more likely to bring Johnny around than punishment.

At this point in the experiment, a late member (an individual who is part of the team of experimenters) joins the group. This newcomer advocates punishment—not the severest possible, but strong enough to get Johnny to recognize the inappropriateness of his ways. The original seven participants do not know that the punishment advocate has been instructed to adopt that position as part of the experiment. (This fact is revealed only later in the experiment.)

When the late member joins the group, attention shifts in a dramatic way. The group attitude is clear: this new member must be persuaded that punishment is inappropriate. The other members communicate with the dissenter, expressing a variety of arguments to persuade him or her to come around to their point of view. Few try to probe his position or to understand his reasons, and there is no serious effort to examine a solution different from the one they have already agreed on.

Once arguments against the punishment approach have been exhausted and the punishment advocate continues to maintain an independent position, the seven turn away from the dissenter. They agree among themselves on the love treatment and act as though the punishment advocate no longer exists. Thus the dissenter is effectively isolated; the group goes about its business and ceases directing communication toward this person. In short, when a dissenter member refuses to change his or her position, he or she is ignored.

Since there is no "right" answer, this experiment shows how pressures to **conform** are applied when judgments are subjective. It also examines another question: How much do participants like or dislike the dissenter? The issue of acceptance versus rejection is basic to **cohesion**, people's desire to reinforce bonds within their group.

In the next phase of the experiment, group members are told that the group will be meeting again but must reduce its size. The members are asked to rank all other people in the group for preference of inclusion in another discussion, unrelated to the Johnny Rocco case. The nominations are studied for the frequency with which each of the group members is eliminated from future membership. The question is whether the group members will accept the advocate of punishment as often as they accept the advocates of love. If they do, then the factor of cohesion—that like-minded people enjoy one another—is disproved.

The empirical result is that the person advocating punishment is left out of membership in a future group significantly more often than representatives of the love approach. In fact, people do prefer others who agree with them; they select people who will, through conforming, reinforce the group cohesion. The dissenter, though ignored after he or she fails to be persuaded, is not forgotten; he or she is actively rejected from membership in future groups.

This experiment reveals a basic aspect of group dynamics that operates to enforce conformity: The price of continued deviation from a group norm is rejection. Other studies reveal that this finding holds true not only when opinions differ from those of the majority, but also when abilities are out of line or when emotions are different.

Blake and Mouton go on to assert that because of the negative consequences that flow from expressing convictions that deviate from the norm, people may hide their true feelings and express those that support the group norm. A case similar to that of Johnny Rocco was used to study participant judgments when they were led to believe that the majority of the group had taken a different position from theirs. This study revealed that greater convergence occurs when a group member believes that his or her opinion will be made public than when it is to be kept private. In addition, there is greater convergence if the member believes that there is a possibility of rejection from the group. The results suggest that anticipated group pressures act on a person as though they were real.

## Making Conformity and Cohesion Work For You

Just as norms themselves are neither good nor bad, convergence, conformity, and cohesion can work either for you or against you depending on the team's standards. The next section will look at how you can avoid the pitfalls of converging on counterproductive norms and instead encourage high-functioning 9,9 norms.

## Changing Team and Organizational Norms

*Many years ago, the airline industry established that 60% to 80% of errors in the air could be attributed to failed human interaction. Why should that be the case? The commercial airline industry grew most quickly in the years following World War II. At that time, many military pilots went on to become commercial airline pilots, bringing with them norms that were destructive to group problem-solving: defensiveness, single-loop learning patterns, and mental models built around individual skill and responsibility.*

*In 1978, a United Airlines pilot refused to consider inputs from his crew, resulting in a fatal crash. United concluded that developing non-defensive problem-solving skills was a critical factor in improving safety in the air. A modern airliner is no place to have a defensive pilot who centralizes control in a crisis and fails to use all the resources available to him or her when making a decision.*

*United therefore introduced the first "cockpit resource management program" that focused on the behaviors crews use in stressful situations, and trained pilots to problem-solve productively. Within three years of introducing the new program, United had a 70% drop in routine flying errors. In other words, they succeeded in changing the norms by which cockpit teams operated. (This program and subsequent generations of it are now mandated by the Federal Aviation Administration for all U.S. airlines.)*

*In 1989, Life Magazine devoted two pages of close-up photographs to a bandaged Captain Al Haynes, a United Airlines pilot. Haynes, his crew, and an instructor (who was a passenger) managed to land their DC-10 near Sioux City, Iowa, even after a sudden explosion in the rear engine caused the total loss of all hydraulics, including steering control. They saved 184 lives. Captain Haynes identified cockpit resource management training as being a key factor in the outcome of this crisis in the air. He said, "I am thoroughly convinced it worked for us... Nobody hesitated or asked what to do next. We listened to what the other crew members had to say... We had no procedures to follow.... You've got to see if you can come up with an answer together. That's what happened for us."*

In this case, as for every company, improvement in team performance came by changing from the one standard of task-oriented, individual behavior to more team-oriented norms. The lesson is one that every team should take to heart in examining its own norms:

- What are our norms?

- What norms do we want to have?

- Which norms should we keep? What new norms do we need to adopt? What old norms do we need to change?

If a team knows what it wants to be and then learns where it really is, the knowledge of the gap provides a strong motivation to change.

## *Identifying Effective Norms*

In a way, creating new norms may appear to be a Catch-22 just like becoming a double-loop learner: it's difficult to instill 9,9 leadership behaviors unless you already have them! Imagine, for instance, trying to change the norms in a team culture that wanted to keep things on an even keel (a 5,5 don't-rock-the-boat mentality). People on those teams would be reluctant to upset the status quo or pass judgment on someone else by providing feedback. Or think about having a renowned task master say, "I want you to give me honest feedback." Would you be the first person to say something critical?

Fortunately, there are some simple steps you can take to bridge the gap between where you, your teams, and your organization are today and where you want to be:

- **Discuss the benefits of double loop learning, and introduce simple feedback or critique sessions as a way to learn from experience.** Ask people to talk about good things the team is doing and things that aren't working well, and to suggest what could be done differently. Or keep it even simpler by asking each person to do a "Benefits and Concerns" (Bs & Cs) check, in which they simply state what they like about working with the team (Benefits) and what their areas of Concern are.

- **Discuss and revise current team norms and ground rules.** Have the team discuss which norms are helping and which are hindering the team. Identify new team norms you'd like to adopt. (Use Table 4, next page, as a starting point.)

- **Develop ways to work through barriers to effectiveness.** Decide as a group what keeps your team from being more effective, and brainstorm creative ways to work through or around those barriers.

When trying to decide what norms would be appropriate for your group, the 9,9 Team Leadership orientation discussed in Part I can serve as a starting point. Table 4 (next page) shows some examples of 9,9 behaviors consistent with creating high-functioning teams.

These types of norms will create an environment with sound communication, non-defensiveness, clear understanding of and agreement on goals by all; mutual trust and respect; willingness to discuss undiscussables; a clear picture of roles; mutual accountability; skill in giving and receiving feedback.

As team members become more comfortable with the notion of providing feedback on the team as a whole, you may want to take the next step and establish a norm where people can call each other on "defensive" behaviors (discounting feedback, ignoring others' viewpoints, etc.). Be careful, though. Critiquing an individual's behavior is much riskier than commenting on the team's behavior. You will have had to develop a lot of trust and respect within the team—and have eliminated a lot of defensive behaviors—before taking this step.

# Table 4: Examples of 9,9 Groups Norms (Habits)

## Setting Goals
- The team discusses its goals
- Differences in members' understanding are resolved
- The whole team commits to the agreed-on goals
- Goals and plans are recorded

## Assigning Accountability
- There is a clear understanding about who is to do what and when
- The team uses tracking measures to ensure that work is completed effectively
- Roles are allocated to take advantage of members' interests and capabilities
- Changes are made in role assignments to improve the team's ability to achieve goals

## Handling Conflict
- People openly and spontaneously bring up differences of opinion
- Individuals handle conflict constructively, see it as a creative tool
- People use inquiry to understand others' views
- People provide reasons for their opinions

## Making Decisions
- Decisions are made on time
- Decisions are made by consensus with a focus on the best solution for everyone
- Decisions are based on business reasons and data
- Everyone on the team is involved in the decision-making process or, at least, fully committed to the decisions made
- Important decisions are revised based on new information

## Meeting Effectively
- Time is managed well
- Priorities are set so that key issues will be addressed first
- Contingency plans document how to reallocate priorities when time is tight
- The team uses regular checks and ground rules to improve meeting efficiency
- Meetings start and stop on time

## Learning/ Feedback
- Formal checks are performed regularly to identify opportunities for improvement
- All members contribute to the formal checks
- Team members suggest improvements at the beginning of the activity or project
- People freely suggest improvements at any time
- Time is set aside for "post" checks at the end of every meeting or activity

## Chapter 7 Summary

- People have habits; organizations have norms.

- Norms have a stronger influence on personal and organizational behavior than most people are aware.

- Effective leaders understand how norms develop and wield that knowledge to replace ineffective or counterproductive norms.

# 8

# Levels of Change

I N THE case studies described in this book, you've seen how difficult it can be for people to change their individual behavior. You can therefore appreciate how much harder it will be to change organizational behavior. That's why we emphasize the need to work on individual mastery first, then broaden your horizon to include coworkers and peers before attempting to achieve wider cultural change. The journey from where you are now to where you want to be must progress from personal growth to organizational effectiveness.

Here are some examples of changes at each of these levels:

### Individual

- Increase self awareness
- Deepen self-management
- Increase personal mastery
- Provide a common language to talk about leadership
- Increase understanding of the power and influence of group norms

## Team

- Harness team talent
- Establish a culture of continuous learning
- Achieve team synergy
- Establish high-performance team norms

## Organization

- Create a framework for a learning organization
- Gain commitment
- Create alignment
- Foster cross-team collaboration
- Create systems to support intended and emergent strategies to drive shareholder value

The sequence of these levels is deliberate. You need to get some experience trying to change your own behavior—which requires input from those immediately around you—then slowly expand within your sphere of influence to affect as much of the organization as you can. If you're a frontline supervisor, obviously your opportunity to create change will be much less than if you're a senior VP or CEO.

No matter how big your actual sphere of influence, be careful as you proceed. A top-down imposition of ideas generates compliance not commitment. A common misconception is that exerting pressure and "taking control" will solve the problem. In fact, often the reverse is the case. A better approach is to recognize the power of the existing attitudes and the norms they drive within the organization, and to use open discussion and feedback to gain buy-in and genuine commitment.

**Start by conducting regular feedback sessions** focused on your own behavior and that of your direct reports: These sessions can reduce self-deception and build a culture of continuous personal improvement. Establish a norm within your immediate team first, then later expand to your department or unit, that giving and receiving constructive personal feedback drives a positive, continuous-learning, 9,9 environment. Realize that the organization will be taking cues from your behavior more than from your words. It is essential that the outputs of these sessions are captured in writing. A simple one-page, three-column document is all that is required (see Figure 17).

**Figure 17: Example Feedback Follow-up Sheet**

| Team Member | Actions to Take | How the Team Will Help |
|---|---|---|
| Marianne | Develop inquiry skills | Give feedback when she moves Into a "telling" mode |
| Stephan | Delegate to subordinates | Karl will act as mentor; others to offer reminders |

**Set specific goals for the team** such as "on our next project, we will measure ourselves on setting goals" or "in the next two months, we will improve our meeting effectiveness." Then talk about how your team currently handles that area, and what you'd like to be able to do better.

**Introduce a continuous focus on the behavioral circle** in any meaningful interaction that takes place within your organization. Thus, addressing behavioral issues will become an integral part of meetings, planning sessions, monthly performance reviews, etc. (i.e., a norm).

Transforming yourself and your organization is tough work. No single feedback or team-building session is going to do the trick in creating a high-functioning 9,9 team. Everyone must *practice* just as a sports team would.

### Chapter 8 Summary

- Developing more effective leadership behaviors will have a profound influence on you, your team or workgroup, and the organization.

- It is best to start on a small scale, looking for ways to improve as an individual (perhaps by involving peers and group members in providing feedback).

- Don't try to implement sweeping change at the organizational level until you fully understand what existing policies, practices, and norms will help or block any change.

# Part II Conclusion

## *Personal and Organizational Effectiveness*

In a multinational company implementing Six Sigma corporate-wide, one division stands out as a wonderful success while another seems to have developed a series of "programs" that are poorly integrated into the everyday running of the business. A similar result is seen in the hospitality industry, where one chain has some hotels with outstanding results and others that are stalled.

An analysis by the top leaders of these companies shows that the Six Sigma Champions in the successful divisions or hotels are very savvy about how to wield their influence. They are clear and consistent in their communication about the priorities associated with the initiative. They work closely with all the leaders in their work units to make sure the Six Sigma initiatives are tied to those leaders' business goals. They discuss barriers with those leaders and change policies or practices where needed to encourage and reward new behaviors; they provide coaching and guidance to others involved in the initiative. As a result, these Champions have created new norms that foster employee commitment to the new methods, and make it likely employees will contribute new ideas because they know their ideas will be carefully analyzed and implemented if feasible.

Interestingly, the Champions of the less-successful initiatives were just as smart as their successful counterparts, at least when it came to understanding what Six Sigma was. They fell short, however, in their ability to integrate Six Sigma into the everyday work of their business unit. Some of them were typical 9,1 leaders, expecting people to follow their lead because of their position. Others simply paid no attention to the behavioral component of implementation at all; they came up with plans and expected others to implement those plans without question.

# # #

In the early 1990s, a multinational consumer products company undertook a program to improve its "people systems." The change in the way management worked together was immediate. As a result of a deep examination of the company's structure (a double-loop check that challenged existing mental models about how the company should operate), management decided that the whole central headquarters (including the jobs of most of the senior management team involved in the decision-making) was simply unnecessary, and that the company could operate more efficiently without the extra layer of bureaucracy. The decision was no reflection on the quality of work done at headquarters—the office was operating with a high degree of collaboration and effectiveness due to extensive leadership training. Still, the decision that was best for the company was to dismantle this office. About 9 months before the change was made, everyone in the office was told of the decision. The company kept staff fully informed along the way, offered jobs in other locations to those who could relocate and good severance packages to those who did not want to move. Everyone cooperated in the transition, and it ended up being a tough thing that was done right.

In contrast, a few years later, the new owners of a global corporation decided that they needed to downsize. One Friday, they simply fired 20% of their workforce with no warning, and without severance for non-union employees. You won't be surprised to learn that despite revenues in the billion dollar range, this company eventually went bankrupt.

# # #

Organizations that implement superficial teamwork training tend to have management processes that look more like young children playing soccer than competent adults running a business. People run about in a group chasing the ball, with little regard for their positions on the playing field. For example, large meetings are the norm because everybody wants to be involved in decision-making and planning, regardless of whether they can influence or are influenced by the decisions.

These superficial attempts at teamwork are prone to other dangers. Organizations have a tendency to swing from a tough 9,1 culture all the way to a soft 1,9 culture. There is a backlash

> *against tyrannical management; "people" manag-*
> *ers are hired; performance management systems*
> *are changed to favor individuals with strong people*
> *skills. Organizations that swing to this extreme see*
> *a different form of conformity setting in: there is just*
> *as much defensiveness as under the 9,1 culture,*
> *except now it's around the importance of looking*
> *after people and maintaining harmony among the*
> *troops.*

In their quest for ever-greater performance and results, leaders at all levels have traditionally turned to management theories, processes and techniques to help them solve strategic problems, develop a vision, or improve the quality of their systems. Yet many of these same managers are reluctant to make use of proven behavioral theories and practices to help them solve some of the most intractable problems they face, those that concern the "people" issues.

This reluctance is partly rooted in the discomfort many individuals feel in dealing with personal relationships in a work setting. Many organizations still have a culture where tough-minded individualism, the hero syndrome, is revered and rewarded. There is an antipathy towards consideration for people: "soft issues" are seen as a necessary evil to be endured or even sacrificed to achieve results at all costs.

The Preface described the growing body of knowledge that forms the underlying premise of this book: leaders who are able to understand and shape behavior will be more effective in the long run than those who focus solely on strategy or even on the technical aspects of execution. They use their understanding of behavior to drive both strategy and execution (Figure 18):

**Figure 18: The Third Circle**

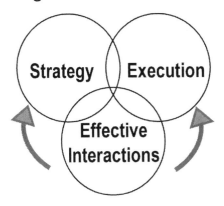

*Creating behaviors that foster
learning and growth*

Effective leaders at every level can work to improve the effectiveness of interactions in their organization:

- Using the Grid and double-loop learning to understand their own strengths and weaknesses

- Using the Johari Window concept to learn more about themselves and allow others to participate in shaping their knowledge and decisions

- Becoming a role model within their spheres of influence; creating environments within those spheres that encourage ideas and feedback

- Understanding the influence of group norms and how they are formed, and reshaping those norms to support 9,9 leadership behavior by all employees within their sphere of influence

We take these steps not just to feel good about ourselves. We take them because they work. Implementing these changes in ourselves, our teams, and our organization will have a profound effect on the organization's ability to achieve its goals and remain competitive. Ineffective leaders, such as the "CEOs who fail," remain mired in denial about themselves and others. They're stuck in single-loop learning, trapped by their own limited perceptions and knowledge.

## Sustaining Organizational Level Change

The issue of achieving and sustaining change at the organizational level is one of the most important challenges any executive faces. For example, when hired by a new company, executives are inevitably confronted with well-entrenched norms: "this is the way we do things around here." People are rarely open to hearing criticisms or suggestions from outsiders. It may be clear to the new manager what needs to be done, but the established culture is entrenched in its existing way of doing things.

Leaders handle this challenge in a variety of ways. Some clean house, bringing in new people—especially in pivotal roles—to replace the old guard; others adopt superficial change-management processes, hiring outside consultants to make the change for them. Research and our personal experience shows that both of these approaches usually yield disappointing results.

An approach that requires more effort in the short run but is far more effective in the long run is to develop expertise in managing your sphere of influence and redefining organizational norms. Recognize that you can take control of your culture's strong silent hand and mold it to produce excellence. Take steps to educate your organization on the richness of research available to them in this arena. Use these ideas in establishing policies. Conduct training to increase inquiry skills and the ability to implement Model II assumptions as part of the culture of your organization. These strategies allow you to use your power and authority as a leader as a positive force that enhances rather than obstructs organizational effectiveness.

A CEO of an organization that is doing it right stated this clearly at a meeting of senior managers. He explained:

> The way we are going to become a great company is to create value for our customers and our shareholders through your efforts at improving how we run every aspect of our business. It is through your efforts that our new product development processes will be improved to deliver better products that satisfy our customers' needs. It is through your efforts that sales and marketing processes will be improved. It is through your efforts that processes will be improved so we can reduce our investment in inventories and accounts receivable.
>
> In our capitalist system (and we haven't come up with a better one yet), the scorecard we are measured against is our financial results. This may not be perfect, but it's the way the system works. If we do a good job it will be reflected in our results. As we choose projects to improve our business we will continually be managing the tension between

*the short-term and the long-term, and between running our business, while at the same time improving it.*

# Bibliography

**Argyris, Chris**

"Teaching Smart People How to Learn," *Harvard Business Review*, Harvard Business School Press, Jan 2002

*Flawed Advice and the Management Trap: How Managers can know when they're getting good advice and when they're not.* Oxford University Press, 1999

*Organizational Learning II: Theory, Method, and Practice* (2nd ed.) [with Donald Schon, Michael Payne], Addison-Wesley Publishing Co., 1996

*Knowledge for Action.* Jossey-Bass, 1993

*Overcoming Organizational Defenses: Facilitating Organizational Learning.* Allyn & Bacon, 1990

**Bass, Bernard M.**

*Transformational Leadership: Industrial, Military, and Educational Impact.* Lawrence Erlbaum Associates, Inc. 1988

**Belbin, Meredith**

*Management Teams: Why They Succeed or Fail.* Butterworth-Heinemann, 1996

*Team Roles at Work.* Butterworth-Heinemann, 1996 (reprint edition)

**Bennis, Warren**

*On Becoming a Leader.* Perseus Press, 1994

*Leaders: Strategies for Taking Charge* [Nanus, Burt (contributor) et al.], Harperbusiness, 1997

**Blake, Robert**

*Leadership Dilemmas-Grid Solutions* [with Anne Adams McCanse], Gulf Professional Publishing Company, 1991

Productivity: The Human Side [with Jane S. Mouton], AMACOM, 1982.

## Charan, Ram and Geoffrey Colvin

"What CEOs Fail." *Fortune* 6/21/1999.

## Curren, Tom

see http://www.topteamalignment.com/whyfail.html

## Collins, James

*Good to Great: Why some companies make the leap and others don't.* HarperCollins. 2001.

*Built to Last: Successful Habits of Visionary Companies* [with Jerry I Porras], Harperbusiness. 1997

## Gardner, Howard

*Intelligence Reframed: Multiple Intelligences for the 21st Century.* Basic Books. 2000

*Frames of Mind: The Theory of Multiple Intelligences.* Basic Books, 1993

*Multiple Intelligences: The Theory In Practice.* Basic Books, 1993

## Luft, Joseph [namesake of the Johari Window, along with Harry Ingham]

*Group Process: An Introduction to Group Dynamics.* Mayfield Publishing Co., 1984.

## Mintzberg, Henry

*The Rise and Fall of Strategic Planning: Reconceiving Roles for Planning, Plans, and Planners.* Free Press, 1993

# Index

Argyris, Chris (and the Argyris Model), 14, 15, 16, 18, 20, 21, 22, 54, 74

Assumptions
Model I, 16, 17, 21–24, 54, 55, 73, 78, 96
Model II, 18–22, 24, 51, 55, 74, 139

Avolio, Bruce, 61–63

Bass, Bernard M., 61–63

behavior, 3, 5, 72, 111

Belbin, Meredith, 104, 106

Bennis, Warren, 60

Blake, Robert (see also Managerial Grid), 28, 47, 111, 112, 117–120, 122

case studies
attempt to quantify leadership, 59
Bill, the bureaucrat, 79
Carl, the well intentioned CEO who struggles with double loop learning, 69
CEO at workshop, 13
changing cockpit norms, 123
chemical plant with bad norms, 111
Chuck the impoverished leader, 43
company with spotty success at Six Sigma, 133
consumer products company trying to improve its people systems, 134
dot.com with Ph.D. techies, 83
Irene, the new president who sees significant differences in her direct reports (managing sphere of influence), 100
Jessica, the paternalistic leader, 38
Johnny Rocco, case used to demonstrate cohesion, 120
Kathy, the schmoozing CEO (managing sphere of influence), 100
Larry, the country club leader, 34
Marsha and the VP, 11
Miguel, the team leader, 50

case studies, cont.

    Miriam, who manages her sphere of influence, 103, 109

    Nathan, the newly promoted supervisor (managing sphere of influence), 99

    Randy, who learns his changes have made a difference, 95

    Susan, the sincere but controlling manager, 96

    Tim, with the closed Johari window, 83-85, 89-91

    Tony, the sr. exec open to feedback, 76–78

    Victor adopts a new mindset, 14–15, 18

Change, sustaining, 138

Charan, Ram, 1–3

cohesion, 117, 120, 121, 123

Collins, James, 64–65

    levels of leadership, 64

Colvin, Geoffrey, 1–3

Concern (see also Managerial Grid)

    for people, defined  28, 114

    for production, defined 27, 114

conformity, 117, 120, 122, 123, 136

convergence, 117, 119, 120, 122, 123

Curren, Tom, 1-3

defensiveness, 16-18, 20–23,55, 57, 63, 65, 90, 109, 124, 128, 136

execution, 2–4, 137

externalization, 37

Gardner, Howard, 63, 64

Interactions, behavioral, 3, 4, 29, 83, 137

Johari Window, 84–89, 109, 137

leaders/leadership (see also Managerial Grid)
    laissez-faire, 61
    leadership, 2, 6, 27, 57, 59, 60-67
    dynamic approach, 65-66
    prescriptive approach, 65
    transactional, 61
    transformational, 61

learning, 14, 65, 127, 131
    about behavior, 72-79
    double-loop, 22, 24, 56, 62, 63, 74-75, 79, 126, 137
    catch-22, 74
    single-loop, 20-21, 54, 56, 138

Managerial Grid, 28-57, 63, 114, 137
    1,1 impoverished leader, 43–46
    summary of, 45-46
    1,9 country club, 34-37, 38, 39, 41, 50, 52, 55, 57, 114, 136
    summary of, 37
    5,5 middle-of-the-road, 46–49, 55, 125
    summary of, 49
    9,1 task-oriented, 4, 30–34, 38, 51, 60, 136
    summary of, 34
    9,9 team leader, 39, 50–54, 58, 64–66, 69, 79, 80, 90, 95, 103, 112,
        123–126, 131, 138
    summary of, 54
    9+9 paternalistic, 29, 38–42, 79
    summary of, 42

mental models, 14-20

Mintzberg, Henry, 61

Mouton, Jane Srygley, 28, 47, 111, 112, 117–120, 122

multiple intelligences, 63

norms, 5, 97, 111–128, 138–139
    changing, 123
    good, 125
    how they develop, 117

paternalism, 38, 39

sphere of influence, 100–101, 109, 130, 139

strategy, 1–4, 137

team roles
    Belbin model, 105
    Preferred, 108

Three Circle Model, 3, 90, 96, 137

# Author Information

**Max Isaac** is the CEO of
3Circle Partners. He brings
a depth of knowledge and
experience from his career
in general management and
consulting in North America,
Europe and Asia.

Max has assisted CEOs and
senior leaders within client
organizations with the design and
implementation of Interaction
Planning processes, team based
organizational development
programs, and Lean Six Sigma
initiatives.

Prior to moving into the field of organizational development,
Max was the CFO for the Retail Division within The Molson's
Organization, where he took a lead role in growing the
business to over $1 billion in revenues, doubling its size in four
years through acquisitions and internal growth.

Max is the co-author of *Close the Interaction Gap*, *The Third
Circle: Interactions That Drive Results*, *Setting Teams Up for Success*,
and *A Guide to Team Roles*. He is also the contributing author
of the organizational change sections of Mike George's books
*Lean Six Sigma* and *Lean Six Sigma for Service*. Max is a registered
CPA, CA. in Canada. His undergraduate degree was earned at
Witwatersrand University, South Africa.

**Anton McBurnie** has developed a unique international perspective from working in, and consulting to, organizations in Europe, Asia and North America. He has a wealth of experience in the areas of effective leadership, team performance and achieving sustainable results with a specific focus on how the Executive & Senior Teams of an organization drive success in these areas.

Co-author of *Close The Interaction Gap* and *The Third Circle: Interactions That Drive Results*, Anton is a strong communicator who can motivate and bring diverse teams together to achieve a common goal. His current role with 3Circle Partners includes consulting and advising select client organizations, business development and overseeing international growth.

His career has taken him from marketing and brand management positions with Proctor & Gamble in the UK, and Consol Glass in South Africa to general management roles with L'Oreal in France, Hong Kong and Japan. Before moving into consulting, Anton's previous positions in North America included Managing Director of the Canadian affiliate of Estée Lauder Cosmetics; President of Sparks.com, an Internet start-up; and C.O.O. of Premier Salons International, a 1500-unit retail chain of beauty salons.

Anton earned his MBA from the London Business School and his BSc in Zoology & Psychology from the University of Exeter, England.

# What is poor interaction costing you?

Effectiveness in today's workplace relies on how well people can pool their talents, resources, and knowledge to achieve results. Data from 3Circle Partners demonstrate there is a big gap between what people and groups actually achieve and what they could achieve if they could interact more effectively.

*Close the Interaction Gap* explores the most common causes of interaction gaps and provides practical steps for improving the effectiveness of individuals, groups, and organizations.

Learn more at 3CirclePartners.com.

Made in the USA
Columbia, SC
01 February 2018